How to Mix
The World's Best
Cocktails

Featuring the
photography of
Peter Barry

Text by
Helen Spence

Designed by
Philip Clucas MSIAD

Produced by
Ted Smart and **David Gibbon**

How to Mix
The World's Best
Cocktails

COLOUR LIBRARY BOOKS

Contents

FIRST WORDS

'Shaken or stirred?', a question dating back half a century to the days when every home entertainer possessed at least one cocktail shaker, and a very well-stocked bar. The last few years have witnessed the resurrection of the cocktail – along with all its associated paraphernalia. The revival has been accompanied by an enthusiastic interest in the composition of the concoctions themselves, and this book aims to provide the answers to the questions asked by anyone wishing to try their hand at cocktail-mixing.

YOU WILL NEED . . .

Most of the equipment used by the cocktail bartender can be improvised from basic kitchen tools. It is, however, worth investing in a simple stainless-steel *cocktail shaker* – although you can use a wide-mouthed fruit juice bottle with a screw-top lid. A *mixing glass* or a plain glass jug with a two pint capacity is needed to make any drink which requires stirring with ice. The stirrer is ideally a long-handled *barspoon*, and the drink, once chilled, is poured through a *cocktail or 'Hawthorne' strainer*. Any of the more exotic concoctions – particularly those made with fresh fruit – as well as drinks which incorporate eggs or cream are best made in an *electric blender*. Most cocktail bars use heavy-duty blenders designed for breaking up ice cubes, but the household blender works more efficiently if the ice is crushed (see page 9) before it is blended.

A *refrigerator* is essential – a warm cocktail is nasty. Keep the freezer compartment filled with ice trays and, where possible, use ice straight from the freezer. Otherwise store the ice in a well-insulated *ice bucket*.

All cocktails should be carefully measured, and as long as the *measure* remains constant throughout a recipe, the drink will have the correct flavour and consistency. A sharp *fruit knife* and a *chopping board* should be available for slicing garnishes and making twists of citrus peel (see page 9), and a *lemon squeezer* will be needed to extract lemon, lime and orange juices. You will increase the yield of citrus juice by soaking the fruit in hot water for a few minutes before squeezing it.

There are numerous other tools of the trade which are fun to collect, but armed with the equipment listed above, you should be able to mix any cocktail.

GLASSES

Almost any receptacle, from a brandy balloon to a pineapple shell, can be made to work effectively, provided that it is convincingly presented. As a rough guideline, however, choose stemmed glasses for cocktails which are not served on ice, as they will stay cool longer, and tumblers or highball glasses for rocks drinks. Short cocktails look their best in traditional triangular cocktail glasses, while goblet styles are generally used for drinks incorporating egg yolks.

All cocktails are served very cold and it makes a tremendous difference if the glasses have been chilled. Ideally, the glasses should stand in the refrigerator for an hour or two before needed, but a scoop of ice placed in the glass, and left there while the drink is being prepared, will chill it very efficiently.

GARNISHES

A garnish should enhance a drink without disguising it. It can be anything from a creamy-white orchid floating on an exotic frappéed concoction, to a stuffed green olive, speared on a cocktail stick and submerged in a classic Dry Martini.

Slices of lemon, orange and lime are the most frequently used garnishes, along with cocktail cherries which, incidentally, look prettier threaded on coloured cocktail sticks than merely dropped into the drink.

Let your imagination run riot when garnishing tropical cocktails, for truly beautiful creations can be dreamed up using exotic fruits like pineapple, mango or kiwi fruit.

One stylish method of decoration uses the fruit to reflect the ingredients of the drink – apricot wedges on the rim of the Apricot Sour glass, strawberries in a Strawberry Dawn or slices of peach with a Peach Daiquiri. Never go overboard, however, or the drink will look like a fruit salad.

Savoury garnishes include pearl onions, cucumber slices and slivers of the dark green skin,

celery sticks, stuffed olives and sprigs of fresh mint. Celery salt and paprika are sometimes sprinkled over the finished drink before serving.

A pretty way to enhance a sweet cocktail is to frost the rim of the glass with sugar. First dip the rim into a saucer of egg white and then into one of finely granulated sugar. A pink frosting can be achieved by substituting grenadine for egg white. A Margarita is usually served in a salt-frosted glass. To salt the rim, hold the glass upside down and run a wedge of lime or lemon around it. Dip it in a saucer of salt and shake off the excess. Label sugar and salt clearly!

Cream and egg mixtures are flattered by a light dusting of freshly grated nutmeg or powdered cinnamon, while blanched almonds and crystallised stem ginger are both unusual and appealing when used with a little flair. Tropical cocktails look extra-special if frivolous extravagances such as coloured paper parasols are added, and straws come in all sorts of colours, shapes and sizes, and it is worth having a good selection. Never overdress a drink as it simply looks silly, but tantalise both the eye and the palate and you will have a successful cocktail.

TO MEASURE

Provided that the measure used is consistent throughout any one recipe, the drink will have the correct flavour, texture and colour. I have listed the ingredients as ratios which means that any measure, from a teaspoon to an egg cup, can be used effectively, depending on the size of, or number of drinks required.

A Savoy 90 (p.100) served in a sugar-rimmed glass.

TO SHAKE

If a recipe indicates that a drink is to be shaken, put the ingredients together with plenty of ice into the shaker and shake rapidly, with a vertical movement, until the outside of the shaker is frosty. Always strain unless specifically directed otherwise. NEVER shake fizzy ingredients – they are always added afterwards.

TO STIR

If a recipe indicates that a drink is to be stirred, add the ingredients to ice cubes in a mixing glass, stir with a long-handled barspoon, and strain.

TO BLEND

Blend the ingredients stated with the recommended amount of crushed ice, and for only a few seconds or the drink becomes weak and watery.

TO MAKE 'GOMME' SYRUP

Dissolve a cup of white sugar in a cup of water by slowly bringing them to the boil and simmering for a couple of minutes. When cool, decant the sugar syrup into a bottle, label and store in a refrigerator.

TO EXTRACT CITRUS JUICE

Fresh fruit juice is infinitely better than bottled or canned, and to extract as much juice as possible from the fruit, soak for a few minutes in hot water before squeezing.

USING EGG WHITE

Egg white does not alter the flavour of a drink, it simply enhances its appearance, and only needs to be used in very small quantities. Separate one or two egg whites into a jug and literally 'cut' them with a sharp knife. This will prevent the whole lot slipping into the shaker when you only want a dash. (Keeps for two days if stored, covered, in a refrigerator.)

FLOATING A LIQUEUR

To float Galliano on a Harvey Wallbanger (see page 60) for example, pour the liqueur into a dessert spoon, hold the bowl of the spoon just above the drink and gently tip it so that the liqueur slips slowly onto the surface.

TO MAKE A TWIST OF PEEL

Using a very sharp knife, shave off strips of the coloured part of the peel leaving behind the white pith. Twist a strip of peel over the surface of the drink, which will release a fine spray of essential oil into the glass. Then drop the twist into the cocktail.

TO SERVE

Always hold the glass by the stem or the base to avoid fingerprints and unnecessary warming of the drink. Never fill the glass to the brim, and remember to leave room for a garnish if one is to be used.

TO MAKE CRUSHED ICE

Wrap ice cubes in a clean, dry tea towel and bash with a mallet.

Key to symbols used in text:

Old fashioned

Goblet

Champagne flute

Cocktail glass

Highball

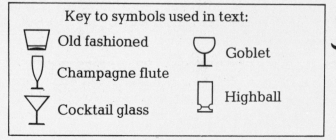

A selection of brandy-based drinks are illustrated here. The Horse's Neck (far left) is a long drink made with brandy and ginger ale, decorated with a spiral of lime peel. The easiest way to make a spiral of citrus peel is by using a conventional apple peeler: draw the blade slowly around the fruit taking a long, thin strip of the coloured zest, which can be anchored in the glass with ice cubes, the other end being allowed to curl over the rim. A Prince Charles (second from left) combines equal quantities of brandy, Drambuie and lemon juice – the mix being shaken to achieve the cloudy, slightly frothy effect. The Stinger (third from left) is an extraordinary blend of brandy and white crème de menthe – try it and see…Cointreau and lemon juice are added to brandy to make the Sidecar (third from right), one of the cocktail 'greats', while another citrus-flavoured concoction is the Brandy Crusta (second from right). Finally, a traditional Egg Nog (far right) is not only nutritious, incorporating milk and a whole egg, but it packs quite a punch with a measure each of brandy and rum.

BRANDY

The Grape that can with Logic absolute
The Two-and-Seventy jarring Sects confute:
The sovereign Alchemist that in a trice
Life's leaden metal into Gold transmute.
Omar Khayyam

Brandy is a spirit distilled from the fermented juices of
grapes, and the word 'brandy' generally implies a grape
distillate – fruit brandies like cherry and peach always
indicate their fruit on the label. The finest of all grape
brandies is cognac, which comes from the Charente
region of France. Armagnac, named after the region to
the south-west of the Charente, is another excellent
brandy. It is not necessary, however, to use the best
cognacs or armagnacs in cocktail mixing – the younger,
less expensive brandies can be used very successfully,
as can those from countries other than France,
such as Greece, Spain or Italy.

ALEXANDER ⅋

Shake together equal parts of brandy, brown crème de cacao and cream, and dust with freshly-grated nutmeg.

AMERICAN BEAUTY ⅋

Shake together equal parts of brandy, grenadine, dry vermouth and orange juice, and a dash of white crème de menthe. Top with a little port.

BALTIMORE EGG NOG ⅋

Shake together two parts brandy, two parts Madeira, one part dark rum, two parts milk, an egg and a teaspoon of gomme syrup. Dust with grated nutmeg.

BANANA BLISS ⅋

Stir one part brandy with one part crème de banane.

BANDOS WOBBLER ⅋

A speciality of the Sand Bar, Bandos Island, Republic of the Maldives.
Shake together one part cognac, one part Campari, one part dark rum, one part orange juice and a dash of grenadine.

BETWEEN-THE-SHEETS ⅋

Shake together one part brandy, one part white rum, one part Cointreau and a dash of lemon juice.

BILLY HAMILTON ⅋

Shake together one part brandy, one part orange curaçao, one part brown crème de cacao and a dash of egg white.

BOMBAY ⅋

Stir two parts brandy with one part dry vermouth, one part sweet vermouth, a dash of pastis and a couple of dashes of orange curaçao.

BOSOM CARESSER ⅋

Shake together two parts brandy, one part orange curaçao, an egg yolk and a teaspoon of grenadine.

BRANDY (1) ⅋

Stir four parts brandy with one part sweet vermouth and a dash of Angostura bitters.

BRANDY (2) ⅋

Stir four parts brandy with one part orange

Above: a golden cocktail called Between-the-Sheets.

curaçao and a couple of dashes of Angostura bitters. Garnish with a cherry.

BRANDY CRUSTA ⌣

Shake together three parts brandy, one part orange curaçao, three dashes of maraschino, a dash of lemon juice and a dash of Angostura bitters. Serve with straws in a sugar-frosted glass, garnished with a cherry.

BRANDY FLIP ⅋

Shake a measure of brandy with a whole egg and a teaspoon of gomme syrup. Dust with grated nutmeg.

BRANDY GUMP ⅋

Shake together one part brandy, one part lemon juice and a couple of dashes of grenadine.

Above and facing page: American Beauty.

BRANDY PUNCH ⅋

Over a scoop of crushed ice, pour a measure of brandy and four dashes of curaçao. Stir, top up with dry ginger ale, and garnish with a sprig of mint and a slice of orange.

BRANDY BASED

Opposite page and far left: the colourful Carnival.

BREAKFAST NOG ⚲

Shake together one part brandy, one part orange curaçao, one egg and two parts milk. Dust with grated nutmeg.

CARNIVAL ⚲

Shake together equal parts brandy, apricot brandy and Lillet, a dash of kirsch and a dash of orange juice.

CHAMPS ELYSÉES ⚲

Shake together three parts brandy, one part yellow Chartreuse, one part lemon juice and a dash of Angostura bitters.

CHERRY BLOSSOM ⚲

Shake together two parts brandy, three parts cherry brandy, a dash of curaçao, a dash of grenadine and a dash of lemon juice.

CHOCOLATE SOLDIER ⚲

Shake together equal parts brandy, dry vermouth and crème de cacao, and a couple of dashes of orange bitters.

CLASSIC ⚲

Shake together three parts brandy, one part lemon juice, one part orange curaçao and one part maraschino. Serve in a sugar-frosted glass with a twist of lemon peel.

COOL BREEZE ⚲

Shake together two parts brandy, one part Grand Marnier, six parts cream, a couple of dashes of maraschino cherry juice and a dash of Angostura bitters.

CUBAN ⚲

Shake together two parts brandy, one part apricot brandy and one part fresh lime juice.

Top: Chocolate Soldier; near left above: Cool Breeze; above: Classic.

'Claret is the liquor for boys; port for men; but he who aspires to be a hero must drink brandy.' Samuel Johnson

And if, as an aspiring hero or heroine, you cannot face neat brandy, here is a delicious alternative: the Green Room cocktail. To make it, place several ice cubes in a mixing glass and add a measure of brandy, two measures of dry vermouth and a couple of dashes of orange curaçao. Stir the mixture until it is well chilled, and strain it into a classic cocktail glass. Traditionally, the 'green room' is the retiring room of theatrical actors and performers when they are offstage. The name is derived from the days when the walls of the room actually were painted green, a colour which provides a soothing environment which presumably helped to soothe and calm frayed nerves.

DEPTH CHARGE ▽

Shake together one part brandy, one part calvados, a couple of dashes of grenadine and four dashes of lemon juice.

EGG NOG ▽

Shake together one part brandy, one part dark rum, one egg and one tablespoon of gomme syrup. Pour into a goblet, stir in two parts milk, and dust with grated nutmeg.

EGG SOUR ▽

Shake together one part brandy, one part orange curaçao, the juice of a lemon, an egg and a teaspoon of gomme syrup.

*Above: Horse's Neck;
opposite page and
right: a creamy
Alexander (p.12).*

FERNET ▽

Stir one part brandy with one part Fernet Branca, a dash of Angostura bitters and a couple of dashes of gomme syrup. Add a twist of lemon peel.

FIRST NIGHT ▽

Shake together two parts brandy, one part Van der Hum, one part Tia Maria and a teaspoon of cream.

GOLDEN GLEAM ▽

Shake together two parts brandy, two parts Grand Marnier, one part lemon juice and one part orange juice.

GOLDEN MEDALLION ▽

Shake together equal parts brandy, Galliano and fresh orange juice, and a dash of egg white. Grate a little zest of orange over the drink.

GREEN ROOM ▽

Stir one part brandy with two parts dry vermouth and two dashes of orange curaçao.

HARVARD ▽

Stir equal parts brandy and sweet vermouth with a couple of dashes of Angostura bitters and a dash of gomme syrup. Add a twist of lemon peel.

HOOPLA ▽

Shake together equal parts brandy, Cointreau, Lillet and lemon juice.

HORSE'S NECK 🥃

Drop a lemon spiral into a tall glass, anchor with ice cubes, add a measure of brandy and top with dry ginger ale.

LEVIATHAN ▽

Shake together two parts brandy, one part sweet vermouth and one part orange juice.

MINT ROYAL ▽

Shake together equal parts brandy, Royal Mint Chocolate Liqueur and lemon juice, and an egg white.

MONTANA ▽

Stir one part brandy with one part dry vermouth, two dashes of port, two dashes of Angostura bitters and two dashes of anisette.

MORNING GLORY ▽

Shake together two parts brandy, one part orange curaçao, one part lemon juice, and a couple of dashes each of Angostura bitters and pastis. Add a twist of lemon peel.

MOULIN ROUGE 🥃

Over ice cubes pour one part brandy and

four parts pineapple juice. Top up with dry, sparkling wine, stir, and garnish with a cherry and a slice of pineapple.

OLYMPIC

Shake together equal parts brandy, orange curaçao and orange juice.

Right and opposite page: a cool, refreshing Moulin Rouge (p.18), with its brandy kick and bright bubbles of sparkling wine.

The luxurious Ross Royal, above, is a rich, sweet cocktail which combines, in a subtle and unexpected way, the flavours of brandy, banana, mint and chocolate.

PLAYMATE

Shake together equal parts brandy, apricot brandy, Grand Marnier and orange squash, an egg white and a dash of Angostura bitters. Add a twist of orange peel.

PRINCE CHARLES

Shake together equal parts brandy, Drambuie and lemon juice.

RED HACKLE

Shake together two parts brandy, one part Dubonnet and one part grenadine.

ROLLS ROYCE

Shake together equal parts brandy, Cointreau and orange juice.

ROSS ROYAL

Shake together equal parts brandy, crème de banane and Royal Mint Chocolate Liqueur.

SIDECAR

Shake together two parts brandy, one part Cointreau and one part lemon juice.

SLIPSTREAM

Shake together equal parts brandy, Grand Marnier, Lillet and orange juice, an egg white and a couple of dashes of Angostura bitters.

STINGER

Stir two parts brandy with one part white crème de menthe and serve straight up or on the rocks.

THREE MILER

Shake together two parts brandy, one part white rum, a teaspoon of grenadine and a dash of lemon juice.

TNT

Stir two parts brandy with one part orange curaçao, a dash of Angostura bitters and a dash of pastis.

TOREADOR

Shake together two parts brandy, one part Kahlua and a dash of egg white.

WHIP

Shake together equal parts brandy, pastis, dry vermouth and curaçao.

ZOOM

Shake together a measure of brandy, a teaspoon of cream and a teaspoon of honey dissolved in a little hot water.

Gin-based cocktails encompass a wide range of extraordinarily-flavoured and eccentrically-coloured mixtures in addition to the classics like the Dry Martini, the Collins or the White Lady. The Singapore Sling (far left) is a deliciously cooling mix of gin, fresh lemon juice, cherry brandy and soda water – and if fresh mint is available it can be added to make an appetising, aromatic garnish. Gin, vodka, rum, cold tea and cola are an altogether unlikely-sounding combination of ingredients, but they add up to a refreshing Long Island Tea (second from left). The brilliant blue Mediterranean (third from left) is a tempting blend of gin, blue curaçao and lemonade. Sweet and dry vermouths, gin and pineapple juice are shaken together to make the Queens (third from right); while the Negroni (second from right) gets its beautiful glowing colour from Campari and sweet vermouth which are added to gin before topping up the glass with soda water. Beware of the Green Dragon (far right), a wicked concoction of gin, green crème de menthe and Kümmel – slightly diluted with a little lemon juice.

GIN

Gin is the most versatile – and consequently the most popular – of cocktail spirit bases. Its subtle flavour compliments and harmonises with a great variety of other ingredients, and over the years it has almost always been drunk with a mixer. In Thomas Hughes' 'Tom Brown's Schooldays' the dastardly Flashman 'regaled himself on gin punch', while Mr. Bumble in Charles Dickens' 'Oliver Twist' was partial to gin and water.

Gin is a clear, colourless spirit made from grain and flavoured with juniper berries, coriander seeds and a group of ingredients collectively known as botanicals. The word 'gin' derives from geneva – and geneva is not the city in Switzerland but a derivation of genever (the Dutch for juniper) – which in turn comes from the French genevre (now genièvre) which descended from the Latin juniperus! and if all that leaves you in need of a drink – read on…

All the colours of the rainbow ... Western Rose (p.42) below; Alaska, bottom; and the exotic Blue Lady centre below and right.

A1 ⅄

Shake together two parts gin, one part Grand Marnier and a dash of lemon juice. Garnish with a twist of lemon peel.

ALASKA ⅄

Shake together three parts gin and one part yellow Chartreuse.

ALEXANDER ⅄

Shake together equal parts gin, brown crème de cacao and fresh cream, and serve in a sugar-frosted glass.

ANGEL FACE ⅄

Shake together equal parts gin, apricot brandy and calvados.

AURUM COCKTAIL ⅄

Stir one part gin and one part Aurum with two parts sweet vermouth.

BARRIER REEF ⅄

For this evocative cocktail, mix a scoop of vanilla ice cream with one part gin, one part Cointreau and a dash of Angostura bitters. Pour into a glass and splash with a few drops of blue curaçao.

BARTENDER ⅄

Stir equal parts gin, sherry, Dubonnet and dry vermouth with a dash of Grand Marnier.

BERMUDIANA ROSE ⅄

Shake together two parts gin, and one part each of apricot brandy, grenadine and lemon juice.

BLUE BOTTLE ⅄

Stir two parts gin with one part blue curaçao, and one part passion fruit juice.

BLUE JACKET ⅄

Stir two parts gin with one part blue curaçao and one part orange bitters.

BLUE LADY ⅄

Shake together two parts blue curaçao, one part gin, one part fresh lemon juice and a dash of egg white.

BLUE RIBAND ⅄

Stir two parts gin with two parts white curaçao and one part blue curaçao.

BLUE STAR ⅄

Shake together two parts gin, two parts blue curaçao, one part Lillet and one part orange juice.

Opposite: Western Rose (recipe p.42).

BRONX ⅄

Shake together three parts gin and one part each of dry vermouth, sweet vermouth and fresh orange juice.

BRONX TERRACE ⅄

Stir two parts gin with one part dry vermouth and a dash of lime juice cordial, and garnish with a cocktail cherry.

BULLDOG HIGHBALL ⅂

Shake together equal parts gin and orange juice, top up with ginger ale and serve with straws.

BYRRH SPECIAL ⅄

Stir one part gin with one part Byrrh.

CARIBBEAN SUNSET ⅄

Shake together equal parts of gin, crème de banane, blue curaçao, fresh cream and fresh

Opposite: Casino, garnished with a rose.

lemon juice. Pour the creamy-blue mixture into a glass and splash with a little grenadine.

CARUSO ♈

Stir one part gin with one part dry vermouth and one part green crème de menthe.

CASINO ♈

Shake together two parts gin, one part maraschino, one part fresh lemon juice and a dash of orange bitters, and garnish with a cherry.

CINCHER ♈

Stir one part gin with one part cherry brandy and pour over a scoop of crushed ice.

CLARIDGE ♈

Stir two parts gin with two parts dry vermouth and one part each of Cointreau and apricot brandy.

CLOVER CLUB ♈

Shake together three parts gin, one part grenadine, the juice of half a lemon and a dash of egg white. If you replace the egg white with a yolk, the drink becomes a *Clover Club Royal*. A *Clover Leaf* is the same as a Clover Club, but decorated with a sprig of fresh mint.

COASTER ♈

Coat the inside of a glass with Angostura bitters by swirling a few drops round the bowl and tipping out the excess. Add gin to taste and top with soda water.

COLLINS–JOHN or TOM ⌶

Over cracked ice in a tall glass pour the juice of a lemon, a measure of gin and a teaspoon of fine sugar or gomme syrup. Top up with soda water, stir and garnish with a slice of lemon.

CROSS BOW ♈

Shake together equal parts gin, Cointreau and crème de cacao.

Above: Cincher; left above: Crossbow; far left: a green Caruso.

CUPID'S BOW ⅋

Shake together equal parts gin, Forbidden Fruit liqueur, Aurum and passion fruit juice.

DRY MARTINI ⅋

There is no hard and fast rule governing the proportions of gin and dry vermouth which make up this drink. Three parts gin to one part dry vermouth stirred with lots of ice in a mixing glass, strained into a chilled cocktail glass with a plain or stuffed green

Cupid's Bow, facing page and above, is made with rare and exotic ingredients including passion fruit juice and Forbidden Fruit liqueur. Right: Fallen Angel.

olive, and zest of lemon peel squeezed over the top…is delicious. Orange bitters can be added, the ratio can be changed, and the drink can be served on the rocks. The glass can be rinsed out with vermouth and then gin added – you will only discover the most appealing drink by experimenting.

DUBONNET ⅋

Stir together equal parts gin and Dubonnet and add a twist of lemon peel.

DUBONNET ROYAL ⅋

Stir two parts Dubonnet with one part gin, a dash of Angostura bitters and a dash of orange curaçao. Splash with a dash of pastis and decorate with a cherry on a stick.

FAIRY BELLE ⅋

Shake together three parts gin, one part apricot brandy, an egg white and a teaspoon of grenadine.

FALLEN ANGEL ⅋

Shake together three parts gin, one part fresh lemon juice, a couple of dashes of crème de menthe and a dash of Angostura bitters.

FLUFFY DUCK ⊔

Into an ice-filled glass pour two parts gin, two parts advocaat, one part Cointreau and one part orange juice. Stir in soda water to top up and serve with straws.

FORTY EIGHT ⅋

Shake together two parts gin, one part each of apricot brandy, orange curaçao and dry vermouth, and a dash of lemon juice.

FOURTH DEGREE ⅋

Stir equal parts gin, dry vermouth and sweet vermouth, with a couple of dashes of pastis.

FRENCH 75 ⊽

Shake together equal parts gin and fresh lemon juice, and a little gomme syrup. Pour over ice cubes and top up with chilled champagne.

GIBSON ⅋

Basically an extremely dry martini where only a dash of vermouth dilutes the gin – this drink can be served straight up or on the rocks and is garnished with a pearl (silverskin) onion.

GIMLET ⊔

Stir two parts gin with one part lime juice cordial and pour over ice cubes – top up with soda water if a long, sparkling drink is preferred.

GIN AND IT ⅋

Stir equal parts gin and sweet vermouth and garnish with a cherry.

GIN FIZZ ⊽

Shake together a measure of gin, the juice of a lemon and a teaspoon of gomme syrup. Top up with soda water. A *Golden Fizz* is made in the same way, with an egg yolk

The classic Dry Martini (p.28) is shown below, and facing page where it is stylishly served in The Bar at The Ritz.

Far left above: a fire-breathing Green Dragon; above left: the gin-laced Grapefruit.

included at the shaker stage; a *Silver Fizz* includes an egg white, and a *Royal Fizz* is made with a whole egg.

GIN RICKEY

Pour equal parts gin and freshly squeezed lime juice over ice and top up with soda water.

GOLDEN DAWN

Shake together equal parts gin, calvados, apricot brandy and orange juice. Serve splashed with a little grenadine.

GRAPEFRUIT

Shake together equal parts gin and grapefruit juice, and a dash of gomme syrup.

GREEN DRAGON

Shake together four parts gin, two parts green crème de menthe and one part each of Kümmel and lemon juice.

GUARDS

Stir two parts gin with one part sweet vermouth and a splash of orange curaçao.

HAPPY MEDIUM

Shake together two parts gin, two parts Pimm's No. 1, two parts Cointreau, one part Lillet and one part orange squash.

HAVANA

Shake together one part gin, two parts apricot brandy, one part Swedish punsch and a dash of lemon juice.

HAWAIIAN

Shake together equal parts gin and orange juice, and a dash of orange curaçao.

HIBERNIAN SPECIAL

Shake together equal parts gin, Cointreau and green curaçao, and a dash of lemon juice.

INCA

Stir equal parts gin, dry vermouth, sweet vermouth and dry sherry, with a dash of orgeat syrup and a dash of orange bitters.

INSPIRATION

Stir equal parts gin, dry vermouth, calvados and Grand Marnier.

ITZA PARAMOUNT

Stir two parts gin with one part Drambuie and one part Cointreau.

Maiden's Prayer, opposite and right.

Here's to the maiden of bashful fifteen; Here's to the widow of fifty; Here's to the flaunting, extravagant queen; And here's to the housewife that's thrifty. Let the toast pass, – Drink to the lass, I'll warrant she'll prove an excuse for the glass.

Sheridan

JOHN SIMON

Shake together equal parts gin, Grand Marnier, crème de noyau and orange squash, and a dash of Angostura bitters.

LONG ISLAND TEA

Over ice cubes pour one part gin, one part vodka, one part light rum and two parts cold tea. Top up with cola, stir and garnish with a sprig of mint and a slice of lemon.

LUXURY

Shake together two parts gin, one part each of Pimm's No. 1, crème de banane, sweet vermouth and lime juice cordial, and a dash of Angostura bitters.

MAIDEN'S PRAYER

Shake together three parts gin, three parts Cointreau, one part orange juice and one part lemon juice.

MAINBRACE

Shake together equal parts gin, Cointreau and grapefruit juice.

MEDITERRANEAN

Over ice cubes pour two parts gin and one part blue curaçao. Top up with lemonade.

MILLION DOLLAR

Shake together two parts gin, one part sweet vermouth, a teaspoon each of grenadine and pineapple juice, and the white of an egg.

MONKEY GLAND

Shake together three parts gin, two parts orange juice and a couple of dashes each of pastis and grenadine.

NEGRONI

Over ice cubes pour equal parts gin, sweet vermouth and Campari. Garnish with a slice of orange and top up with soda water if required.

OLD ETONIAN

Stir one part gin with one part Lillet, a couple of dashes of crème de noyau and a splash of orange bitters. Garnish with a twist of orange peel.

OPERA

Stir four parts gin with one part Dubonnet and one part maraschino. Garnish with a twist of orange peel.

ORANGE BLOSSOM

Shake together equal parts gin and fresh orange juice.

PALL MALL

Stir equal parts gin, sweet vermouth and dry vermouth with one teaspoon of white

crème de menthe and a couple of dashes of orange bitters.

PARADISE

Shake together two parts gin, one part apricot brandy and one part orange juice.

PARISIAN

Stir two parts gin with two parts dry vermouth and one part crème de cassis.

vermouth, a dash of pastis and a dash of grenadine.

PINK GIN

This is made in the same way as a *Coaster* but served with iced water rather than soda.

PINK LADY

Shake together four parts gin, one part

The alluring Pink Lady is illustrated opposite and below; far right: a Princeton makes an ideal aperitif – strong and stylish; right: a fluffy Perfect Lady.

PERFECT LADY

Shake together two parts gin, one part peach brandy, one part fresh lemon juice and the white of an egg.

PERFECT MARTINI

A less dry martini, this is made with two parts gin and half a part each of dry and sweet vermouth. Stir with plenty of ice in a mixing glass, strain into a stemmed cocktail glass and add a twist of lemon peel.

PICCADILLY

Stir two parts gin with one part dry

grenadine and an egg white. Garnish with a maraschino cherry.

PRINCETON

Stir two parts gin with one part port and a dash of orange bitters. Add a twist of lemon peel.

QUEENS

Shake together equal parts gin, dry vermouth, sweet vermouth and pineapple juice.

RAC

Stir two parts gin with one part each of dry and sweet vermouth, a dash of grenadine

and a dash of orange bitters. Garnish with a twist of orange and a cherry.

Facing page: Pink Gin; below: Red Lion; below right: Royal Arrival; bottom: Saturnus.

RED LION

Shake together two parts gin, two parts Grand Marnier, one part orange juice and one part lemon juice. Serve in a sugar-frosted glass.

REGENT STAR

Shake four parts gin with two parts orange curaçao, one part dry vermouth and one part passion fruit juice.

RESOLUTE

Shake two parts gin with one part lemon juice and one part apricot brandy.

ROADSTER

Shake together equal parts of gin, Grand Marnier and orange juice, and add a twist of lemon peel.

ROYAL ARRIVAL

A speciality of the American Bar, The Savoy Hotel, London.

Shake together ½ gin, ¼ lemon juice, ⅛ Kümmel, ⅛ crème de noyau and a dash of blue food colouring.

ROYAL ROMANCE

Shake together two parts gin, one part Grand Marnier, one part passion fruit juice and a dash of grenadine.

SAKINI

Drier than a dry martini, this drink is made with three parts gin and one part saké, and served straight up with a green olive, or on the rocks.

SALOME

Stir together equal parts of gin, Dubonnet and dry vermouth.

SATAN'S WHISKERS

Shake together equal parts gin, Grand Marnier, dry vermouth, sweet vermouth and orange juice, and a dash of orange bitters.

SATURNUS

Over ice cubes pour one part gin, one part bianco vermouth, two parts crème de banane and four parts orange juice. Top up with chilled champagne.

SHADY GROVE COOLER

Into a tall glass, pour one part gin, one teaspoon gomme syrup and the juice of a lemon. Top up with ginger beer and add ice. Serve with a stirrer.

SIFI FLIP

Shake together two parts gin, one part Cointreau, one part grenadine, one part lemon juice and an egg yolk.

SILVER JUBILEE

Shake together two parts gin, one part crème de banane and one part cream.

SILVER STREAK

Stir three parts gin with two parts Kümmel and serve straight up or on the rocks.

SINGAPORE SLING

Stir two parts gin with one part cherry brandy and one part lemon juice. Pour over ice cubes, add soda water to taste and garnish with a sprig of mint and a slice of orange.

'A lovely lady, garmented in light
From her own beauty'
Percy Bysshe Shelley, 1820

One of the most delicious gin-based cocktails is the classic White Lady. The drink was invented in Paris in 1919, by Harry Mackelhone, founding father of Harry's Bar. It is created by shaking the following ingredients thoroughly with plenty of ice: Two measures of London Dry Gin, one measure of Cointreau, one measure of lemon juice and a dash of egg white. The egg white enhances the appearance of the cocktail by giving it a snowy-white, frothy topping, but it does not affect the flavour. W̶h̶e̶ ̶t̶h̶e̶ ̶shaker is freezing cold, strain the drink into a cocktail glass, and garnish with a maraschino cherry.

SMILING DUCHESS Y

Stir two parts gin with two parts Lillet, one part apricot brandy and one part crème de noyau.

SNAKE-IN-THE-GRASS Y

Shake together equal parts gin, Cointreau, dry vermouth and lemon juice.

STAR DAISY ▭

Shake together two parts gin, two parts calvados, one part fresh lemon juice, a teaspoon of finely granulated sugar or gomme syrup, and a couple of dashes of grenadine. Pour over ice cubes, top up with soda water and garnish extravagantly!

STRAWBERRY DAWN Y

This delicious, summery concoction is made with fresh strawberries: Blend one part gin with one part coconut cream, three fresh strawberries and a couple of scoops of crushed ice – the secret is not to blend for too long or the drink becomes over-diluted. Serve in a large, bowl-shaped glass and stick a strawberry on the rim. To be drunk through short, fat straws.

SWEET MARTINI Y

Stir two parts gin with one part sweet vermouth and garnish with a cherry.

TANGO Y

Shake together two parts gin, one part sweet vermouth, one part dry vermouth, a couple of dashes of orange curaçao and a dash of orange juice.

TRINITY Y

Stir together equal parts gin, sweet vermouth and dry vermouth.

TROPICAL DAWN ▭

Shake two parts gin with two parts fresh orange juice, pour over a scoop of crushed ice and trickle one part Campari over the top. Serve with short straws.

TWENTIETH CENTURY Y

Shake together two parts gin and one part each of crème de cacao, Lillet and lemon juice.

VENETIAN SUNSET Y

Stir two parts gin with one part Grand

Facing page and left: Strawberry Dawn; above: Snake-in-the-Grass; above left: Tropical Dawn.

Below: the frothy and innocent-looking Visitor is deceptively strong.

Above right and facing page: a romantic cocktail for two – the Tango (p.41).

Marnier, one part Campari and one part dry vermouth. Garnish with a cherry.

VISITOR 🍷

Shake together equal parts gin, Cointreau and crème de banane, a dash of orange juice and an egg white.

WESTERN ROSE 🍸

Shake together two parts gin, one part apricot brandy and one part dry vermouth, and a dash of lemon juice.

WHITE HEATHER 🍸

Shake together three parts gin, one part Cointreau, one part dry vermouth and one part pineapple juice.

WHITE LADY 🍸

Shake together two parts gin, one part Cointreau, one part lemon juice and a dash of egg white.

XANTHIA 🍷

Stir together equal parts gin, yellow Chartreuse and cherry brandy.

YELLOW DAISY 🍸

Stir two parts gin with two parts dry vermouth and one part Grand Marnier.

ZA ZA 🍸

Stir equal parts gin and Dubonnet with a dash of Angostura bitters.

These luscious potions are all tropical rum-based concoctions. The Mai Tai (far left), whose name means 'the best' in Tahitian, incorporates rum, lime juice, curaçao and orgeat syrup. The popular Pina Colada (second from left) is a delicious blend of rum, coconut cream and pineapple juice.

The startling Molokai Mike (third from left) is, in effect, one sorbet floated upon another, and although challenging to produce, it is well worth the effort. A graceful, bowl-shaped glass and a perfect gardenia enhance the lethal Scorpion (third from right) which, while being cool, sharp and very refreshing, is also very strong. The scarlet sorbet (second from right) is the La Florida Daiquiri, its colour contrasting with the Blue Hawaiian (far right).

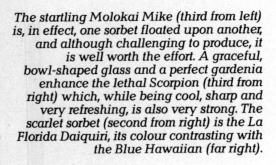

RUM

This '…spirit distilled from fermented sugar-cane juice or from molasses' blends deliciously with fruit juices and liqueurs and is an ideal base for the long, cooling drinks associated with the tropical climates which produce it.

ANTILLANO

Shake together equal parts golden rum, white rum, pineapple juice and grapefruit juice, a dash of Angostura bitters and a teaspoon of grenadine. Pour over crushed ice, garnish imaginatively and serve with fat straws.

The extravagantly-garnished long drink pictured below is an Antillano – summery and refreshing.

APRICOT LADY

Blend together two parts golden rum, two parts apricot brandy, one part fresh lime juice, three dashes of orange curaçao, a couple of dashes of egg white and a small scoop of crushed ice. Serve with a slice of orange and short straws.

BACARDI COCKTAIL

Shake together three parts white rum, one part fresh lemon or lime juice and a few drops of grenadine.

BAHAMAS

Shake together one part white rum, one part Southern Comfort, one part fresh lemon juice and a dash of crème de banane.

BANANA DAIQUIRI

Blend together three parts white rum, one part crème de banane, the juice of half a lime, half a banana and two scoops of crushed ice. Don't blend for too long or the drink will become over-diluted. Pile the icy sorbet into a large goblet and serve with fat straws.

BARRACUDA

Shake together two parts golden rum, one part Galliano, two parts pineapple juice, a couple of dashes of gomme syrup and a good squeeze of lime juice. Serve in a large goblet or, ideally, a pineapple shell, top with champagne and garnish with a slice of lime and a cherry.

BLUE HAWAIIAN

This truly tropical cocktail is made in a blender. Blend together two parts white rum, one part blue curaçao, four parts pineapple juice, two parts coconut cream and a scoop of crushed ice.

A white tuxedo, a white grand piano, and a creamy pink cocktail – what could it be but Casablanca? Pictured facing page and right, this delicious concoction combines the tropical flavours of rum, coconut and pineapple.

BORG SPECIAL

Shake together equal parts Bacardi rum, Drambuie and cherry brandy.

CASABLANCA

Blend together three parts white rum, four parts pineapple juice, two parts coconut cream, a couple of dashes of grenadine and two scoops of crushed ice. Serve with straws.

COCONUT DAIQUIRI

Shake together one part white rum, two parts coconut liqueur, four parts fresh lime juice and a dash of egg white.

CRÈME DE RHUM

Shake together equal parts white rum, crème de banane and orange squash, and a dash of cream. Garnish with a cherry and a slice of orange.

CUBA LIBRE

Over ice cubes pour one part white rum and the juice of half a lime. Drop in the lime shell and stir in cola to taste. Serve with straws.

Opposite page: Palm Breeze (p.50); above: Fireman's Sour; left above: Strawberry Daiquiri (p.54); far left: a soothing Night Light (p.50).

DAIQUIRI

Shake together three parts white rum, one part fresh lime juice and three dashes of gomme (or Falernum) syrup. (If limes are unavailable, substitute lemons.)

DAIQUIRI BLOSSOM

Shake together one part white rum, one part fresh orange juice and a dash of maraschino.

DAIQUIRI LIBERAL

Stir two parts white rum with one part sweet vermouth and a dash of Amer Picon.

DEAN'S GATE

Stir two parts white rum with one part Drambuie and one part lime juice cordial. Add a twist of orange peel.

FIREMAN'S SOUR

Shake together three parts golden rum, two parts fresh lemon juice, one part grenadine and a couple of dashes of gomme syrup.

Add soda water to taste and garnish with a slice of orange and a cherry.

FROSTY DAWN

Shake together two parts white rum, one part maraschino, one part Falernum syrup and two parts orange juice.

FROZEN DAIQUIRI

Blend together one part white rum, a dash of maraschino, the juice of half a lime, a dash of gomme syrup, and two scoops of crushed ice. Serve with fat straws.

JAMAICA JOE

Shake together equal parts Jamaica rum, Tia Maria and advocaat. Add a dash of grenadine and dust with nutmeg.

KING'S DAIQUIRI

Blend together three parts white rum, one part Parfait Amour, one part fresh lime juice, a teaspoon of sugar, a dash of egg white and two scoops of crushed ice.

LA FLORIDA DAIQUIRI

Blend together two measures light rum, one teaspoon gomme syrup or fine sugar, one teaspoon maraschino liqueur, the juice of a lime and a small scoop of crushed ice. Serve with short straws.

Facing page and below right: Planters' Punch (p.52).

LITTLE PRINCESS

Stir one part white rum with one part sweet vermouth.

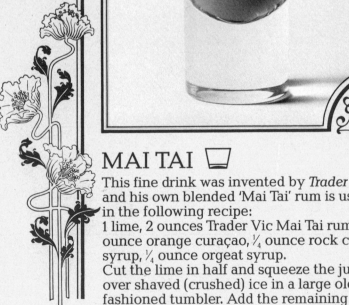

Above: rum, lime juice and cola make a Cuba Libre (p.46).

MAI TAI

This fine drink was invented by *Trader Vic*, and his own blended 'Mai Tai' rum is used in the following recipe:
1 lime, 2 ounces Trader Vic Mai Tai rum, ½ ounce orange curaçao, ¼ ounce rock candy syrup, ¼ ounce orgeat syrup.
Cut the lime in half and squeeze the juice over shaved (crushed) ice in a large old-fashioned tumbler. Add the remaining ingredients and enough shaved ice to fill the glass. Garnish with one spent lime shell, a sprig of fresh mint and a cherry and a pineapple chunk on a stick. Serve with straws. 'Mai Tai' means 'The Best' in Tahitian.

MALLORCA

Stir three parts white rum with one part dry vermouth, one part crème de banane and one part Drambuie.

MARY PICKFORD

Shake together one part white rum, one part pineapple juice, a teaspoon of grenadine and a dash of maraschino.

MOLOKAI MIKE

A *Trader Vic* original.
Blend together 1 ounce orange juice, 1 ounce lemon juice, ½ ounce orgeat syrup, ½ ounce brandy, 1 ounce light rum and one small scoop crushed ice. Pour into glass. Blend together ½ ounce Rhum Negrita, a dash of grenadine and half a scoop crushed ice. Slowly pour into top half of the glass.

MOOMBA COCKTAIL

Shake together three parts white rum, three parts Grand Marnier, two parts orange juice, one part lemon juice and a dash of grenadine. Add a twist of orange peel.

NEVADA

Shake together two parts dark rum, two parts grapefruit juice, one part fresh lime juice and one part gomme syrup.

NIGHT LIGHT

Shake together two parts white rum, one part orange curaçao and an egg yolk.

PALM BREEZE

Shake together three parts dark rum, two parts yellow Chartreuse, one part crème de cacao, the juice of half a fresh lime and a dash of grenadine.

PEACH DAIQUIRI

Blend together three parts white rum, one part peach brandy, the juice of half a lime, half a fresh, peeled peach and two scoops of crushed ice. Pile into a goblet and garnish with a wedge of peach. Serve with short straws.

*Opposite and right:
Shanghai (p.54); far
right: Rum Cooler;
below: Petite Fleur;
bottom: Daiquiri
Blossom (p.49).*

PETITE FLEUR

Shake together equal parts white rum,
Cointreau and fresh grapefruit juice.

PINA COLADA

This is one of the most popular of tropical
cocktails. Blend together three parts white
or golden rum, four parts pineapple juice,
two parts coconut cream and two scoops of
crushed ice. Serve in a tumbler or even
better, a pineapple husk. Garnish with fruit,
paper parasols etc., and two straws.

PINEAPPLE FIZZ

Shake together two parts white rum, one
part pineapple juice and a teaspoon of
gomme syrup. Strain and top up with half
lemonade and half soda water.

PLANTERS

Shake together one part golden rum, one
part orange juice and a dash of fresh lemon
juice.

PLANTERS' PUNCH

Over ice cubes pour one part golden (or
dark) rum, one part fresh lime (or lemon)
juice, a dash of Angostura bitters and two
teaspoons of grenadine. Top up with soda
water and stir. Decorate with slices of
orange and lemon.

RUM COOLER

Shake together one part dark rum, the
juice of a lemon (or lime), and four dashes
of grenadine. Add ice and top up with soda
water.

RUM BASED

RUM NOGG

Shake together one part dark rum, two parts milk, an egg and a teaspoon of gomme syrup. Dust with grated nutmeg.

The sting in the tail of the killer Zombie is the tremendously high percentage of alcohol in the Demararan rum used. There are, in addition, three other rums as well as apricot brandy in the recipe! The Zombie is shown opposite and below. Yellow Bird, right, gets its brilliant colour from the liqueur, Galliano.

SHANGHAI

Shake together four parts dark rum, one part pastis, three parts lemon juice and a couple of dashes of grenadine.

SIX BELLS

Shake together two parts dark rum, one part orange curaçao, one part fresh lime juice, a couple of dashes of Angostura bitters and a dash of gomme syrup.

SMILING IVY

Shake together one part dark rum, one part peach liqueur, one part pineapple juice, a dash of lemon juice and an egg white.

STRAWBERRY DAIQUIRI

Blend together three parts white rum, one part fraise liqueur, the juice of half a lime, three strawberries and two scoops of crushed ice. Pile into a large, bowl-shaped glass and garnish with a strawberry.

SWEET MEMORIES

Stir one part white rum with one part dry vermouth and one part orange curaçao.

TRINIDAD PUNCH

Shake together three parts dark rum, two parts fresh lime juice, a teaspoon of gomme syrup and a couple of dashes of Angostura bitters. Pour over ice cubes, drop in a twist of lemon peel and dust with nutmeg.

XYZ

Shake together two parts golden rum, one part Cointreau and one part lemon juice.

YELLOW BIRD

Shake together three parts white rum, one part Galliano, one part Cointreau and one part fresh lime juice. Do not strain – simply pour into a stemmed glass and garnish with a slice of lime.

ZOMBIE

The world's most lethal cocktail ... Shake together two parts white rum, two parts golden rum, two parts dark rum, one part apricot liqueur, one part pineapple juice, one part lime juice and a dash of gomme syrup. Pour over crushed ice, splash in a little 151 proof Demararan rum, garnish with slices of pineapple, orange, lemon and lime, and serve with straws.

SCORPION

Blend together three parts golden rum, two parts fresh lemon juice, two parts fresh orange juice, one part brandy, a couple of dashes of orgeat syrup and a scoop of crushed ice. Pour the mixture over more crushed ice, garnish with a sprig of mint and a slice of orange and serve with short straws.

The Hong Kong Fizz (far left) is a potent mix of vodka, gin, three liqueurs, lemon juice and soda water. Vodka, Cointreau and lemon juice make a Balalaika (second from left) while the Black Russian (third from left) is a mix of vodka and Kahlua. White crème de menthe and lemonade are added to vodka making a Snake-in-the-Grass (third from right); and a salt-frosted glass is as essential to a Salty Dog (second from right) as Worcestershire sauce is to a Bloody Mary (far right).

VODKA

The word 'vodka' comes from the Russian word for water, 'voda', and, appropriately, vodka is a colourless, odourless and virtually tasteless spirit. It is this very neutrality that makes it such a versatile spirit base, giving a drink a kick without affecting its taste. It is usually distilled from grain rather than potato, and the distillate is very carefully filtered to remove all impurities. It was not until the late 1940s that vodka became a fashionable drink, by which time it had missed the cocktail 'boom'. As a result, there are comparatively few vodka-based cocktail recipes, and many of these are variations on drinks originally made with gin.

ALVEAR PALACE

Shake together five parts vodka, two parts pineapple juice and one part apricot brandy.

APRÈS SKI

Shake together equal parts vodka, green crème de menthe and Pernod. Top up with lemonade, decorate with a sprig of mint and a slice of lemon, and serve with straws.

Above: blue curaçao colours and flavours the Blue Lagoon; right: Après Ski; opposite page: Gipsy (p.60).

BALALAIKA

Shake together equal parts of vodka, Cointreau and lemon juice.

BARBARA

Shake together two parts vodka, one part crème de cacao and one part cream.

BLACK RUSSIAN

Over ice cubes pour two parts vodka and one part Kahlua.

BLENHEIM

Shake together two parts vodka, one part Tia Maria and one part fresh orange juice.

BLOODSHOT

Shake together one part vodka, two parts beef bouillon or condensed consommé, two parts tomato juice, a dash of lemon juice, a couple of dashes of Worcestershire sauce and a pinch of celery salt.

BLOODY MARY

Shake together one part vodka, four parts tomato juice, a couple of dashes of Worcestershire sauce, a dash of lemon juice and a pinch of celery salt. Add Tabasco and pepper to taste and serve with a stick of celery which may be used to stir the drink.

BLUE LAGOON

Over ice cubes pour one part vodka, one part blue curaçao and top up with lemonade.

CHI CHI

Blend together three parts vodka, two parts coconut cream, eight parts pineapple juice and two scoops of crushed ice. Garnish with a slice of fresh pineapple and a cherry and serve with fat straws.

CHOP NUT

Shake together two parts vodka, one part coconut liqueur, one part crème de banane, two parts orange juice and a dash of egg white.

COSSACK

Shake together equal parts vodka, brandy and lime juice, and a teaspoon of gomme syrup.

CZARINE

Stir two parts vodka with one part dry vermouth, one part apricot brandy and a dash of Angostura bitters.

DANIELLI

Stir two parts vodka with one part dry vermouth and a couple of dashes of Campari. Add a twist of lemon peel.

DEB'S DELIGHT

Stir two parts vodka with two parts apricot brandy and one part anisette. Do not strain, but pour liquid and ice into a tumbler and top with cream.

FROZEN STEPPES

Blend together two parts vodka, one part brown crème de cacao and a scoop of vanilla ice cream.

GIPSY ⍙

Shake together two parts vodka, one part Bénédictine and a dash of Angostura bitters.

GODMOTHER ⊔

Over ice cubes pour two parts vodka and one part amaretto.

Bénédictine and lemon juice. Top up with soda water and garnish with slices of lemon, orange and lime, and a cherry.

JUSTINE ⍙

Shake together two parts vodka, one part crème de noyau, one part kirsch, a couple of dashes of orgeat syrup and two parts cream.

Opposite page and below: Harvey Wallbanger; below right: Hong Kong Fizz; far right: Moscow Mule; bottom: Gipsy.

GOLDEN TANG ⍙

Shake together four parts vodka, two parts Strega, one part crème de banane and one part orange squash. Garnish with a cherry.

HARVEY WALLBANGER ⊔

Over ice cubes pour three parts vodka and eight parts orange juice. Float two teaspoons of Galliano on top and garnish with a slice of orange.

HONG KONG FIZZ ⍙

Shake together equal parts of vodka, gin, yellow Chartreuse, green Chartreuse,

KATINKA ⍙

Shake together three parts vodka, two parts apricot brandy and one part fresh lime juice. Pour over a scoop of crushed ice and garnish with a sprig of mint.

LUCKY DIP ⍙

Shake together two parts vodka, one part crème de banane, one part lemon squash and an egg white.

MOSCOW MULE ⊔

Over ice cubes pour two parts vodka and one part fresh lime (or lemon) juice. Stir in

Below: cream-topped Deb's Delight (p.58); below left and facing page: Salty Dog.

ginger beer to top up, garnish with a sprig of mint and a slice of lime, and serve with straws.

ORANGE BLOSSOM

Shake together two parts vodka, two parts apricot brandy, one part Galliano and one part orange juice. Top up with ginger ale, garnish with a slice of orange and a cherry, and serve with straws.

PATRICIA

Stir one part vodka with one part sweet vermouth and one part orange curaçao. Add a twist of lemon peel.

QUIET SUNDAY

Shake together two parts vodka, one part amaretto and eight parts orange juice. Pour into an ice-filled glass and splash in a few drops of grenadine.

ROAD RUNNER

Shake together two parts vodka, one part amaretto and one part coconut milk. Dust with grated nutmeg.

ROBERTA MAY

Shake together equal parts vodka, Aurum and orange squash, and a dash of egg white.

SALTY DOG

Over ice cubes in a salt-frosted glass pour one part vodka and two parts grapefruit juice.

SCOTCH FROG

Shake together two parts vodka, one part Galliano, one part Cointreau, the juice of a lime, a dash of Angostura bitters and a teaspoon of maraschino cherry juice.

VODKA BASED

Facing page and below right: a Vodkatini garnished with a twist of lemon peel; right: SW1; below: Sloe Comfortable Screw.

SCREWDRIVER

Over ice cubes pour one part vodka and four parts orange juice.

SEA BREEZE

Stir three parts vodka with one part dry vermouth, one part blue curaçao and one part Galliano. Pour over ice cubes and add a twist of orange peel.

SERENISSIMA

Shake together one part vodka, one part fresh grapefruit juice and a dash of Campari. Pour into an ice-filled glass.

SILVER SUNSET

Shake together two parts vodka, one part apricot brandy, one part lemon juice, six parts orange juice, a dash of Campari and a dash of egg white. Pour over ice cubes, garnish with a slice of orange and a cherry, and serve with straws.

SLOE COMFORTABLE SCREW

Over ice cubes pour two parts vodka, one part sloe gin, one part Southern Comfort and eight parts fresh orange juice.

SNAKE-IN-THE-GRASS

Over ice cubes pour two parts vodka and one part crème de menthe. Top up with lemonade and garnish with a slice of orange.

SW1

Shake together equal parts vodka, Campari and fresh orange juice, and a dash of egg white.

VODKATINI

As with the gin-based dry Martini, there are countless variations as to the proportions used in this drink. A safe ratio is two parts vodka to one part dry vermouth, to which a twist of lemon peel is added.

YELLOW FINGERS

Shake together two parts vodka, two parts Southern Comfort, two parts orange juice and one part Galliano. Top up with lemonade and garnish with a slice of orange and a maraschino cherry.

Generally speaking, whisky has such a strong flavour that it mixes successfully with a relatively limited number of ingredients. Here are some of the successes…The Frisco Sour (far left) combines bourbon, Bénédictine, lemon and lime juice, and the Maple Leaf (second from left) is actually flavoured with maple syrup. The Angers Rose (third from left) is made by shaking bourbon with Cointreau, Campari, pineapple juice and egg white. A Whisky Sour (third from right) is traditionally made with Scotch, while the Hunter (second from right) and the Old Fashioned (far right) are usually preferred with rye.

WHISKY

The name 'whisky' is derived from 'usquebaugh' or 'uisge beatha', Celtic words meaning 'water of life'. Malt whisky, for which Scotland is justifiably famous, is made from barley which is malted and heated over a peat fire, and it is the smoke from this fire which gives the whisky its distinctive smoky aroma. Pure spring water is added to the flavoured malt, which ferments to a beer; and this is distilled to produce a spirit which is then matured, in oak, for between five and twenty years. Grain whisky, generally made with corn, is cheaper to produce than malt, and its scent and flavour are much milder. The Scotch used in cocktails and mixed drinks is usually a blend of malt and grain whiskies. Irish whiskey is made in a similar way to Scotch, but the malted barley is not smoked, and the whiskey is distilled three times. Light-bodied Canadian whisky, made from corn with added wheat, rye and barley malt, is often called 'rye'. True rye whiskey, however, is made with over 51% rye, and most of it is produced in Maryland and Pennsylvania. Bourbon, aged in charred oak barrels, and made with over 51% corn, is a name which nowadays covers several corn-mash whiskies, although it originated in Bourbon County, Kentucky.

AFFINITY

Stir two parts Scotch with one part sweet vermouth and a couple of dashes of Angostura bitters.

ANGERS ROSE

Shake equal parts bourbon, Cointreau and pineapple juice with a dash of Campari and a dash of egg white. Garnish with a slice of orange and a cherry.

BARBICAN

Shake together seven parts Scotch, one part Drambuie and two parts passion fruit juice.

BOBBY BURNS

Stir one part Scotch with one part sweet vermouth and three dashes of Bénédictine.

BOSTON FLIP

Shake equal parts rye and Madeira with one egg yolk and a teaspoon of gomme syrup.

BOURBONELLA

Stir two parts bourbon with one part dry vermouth, one part orange curaçao and a dash of grenadine.

BROOKLYN

Stir equal parts rye and sweet vermouth with a dash of maraschino and a dash of Amer Picon.

COMMODORE

Shake four parts rye with one part fresh lime juice and two dashes of orange bitters. Add sugar if required.

DAILY MAIL

Shake equal parts rye, Amer Picon and orange squash with three dashes of orange bitters.

DANDY

Stir equal parts rye and Dubonnet with a dash of Angostura bitters and three dashes of Cointreau. Garnish with orange and lemon peel.

EMBASSY ROYAL

Shake together two parts bourbon, one part Drambuie, one part sweet vermouth and two dashes of orange squash.

The Brooklyn, above, uses rye whiskey, whereas the Godfather, facing page and far right, is made with either Scotch or bourbon.

EMPIRE GLORY

Shake together two parts rye, one part ginger wine, one part fresh lemon juice and two dashes of grenadine.

EVANS

Stir a large measure of rye with a dash of apricot brandy and a dash of curaçao.

FORESTERS' DELIGHT

Shake together one part bourbon, one part Cointreau, two dashes of blue curaçao and two dashes of freshly squeezed lemon juice. Serve in a sugar-frosted glass, garnished with a cherry.

FRISCO SOUR

Shake together three parts bourbon, one part Bénédictine, one part fresh lemon juice and one part fresh lime juice. Garnish with slices of lemon and lime.

GODFATHER

Over ice cubes pour two parts Scotch or bourbon and one part amaretto.

HOOTS MON

Stir two parts Scotch with one part Lillet and one part sweet vermouth.

Above: Mint Julep; above right: the Commodore (p.68), traditionally served strained, but seen here served on the rocks; far right and facing page: the original Old Fashioned.

HUNTER

Stir two parts rye with one part cherry brandy.

INK STREET

Shake together equal parts rye, lemon juice and orange juice.

KENTUCKY SUNSET

Stir three parts bourbon with one part Strega and one part anisette. Garnish with a twist of orange peel.

LINSTEAD

Shake together one part Scotch, one part sweetened pineapple juice and a dash of pastis. Garnish with a twist of lemon peel.

LOS ANGELES

Shake together two parts Scotch, one part lemon juice, one egg and a dash of sweet vermouth.

MANHATTAN

The traditional Manhattan is made with two parts rye, one part sweet vermouth and a dash of Angostura bitters, stirred and garnished with a cherry. A Dry Manhattan replaces sweet vermouth with dry and the cherry with a twist of lemon peel; and a Perfect Manhattan uses half sweet and half dry vermouth and is garnished with both a cherry and a twist of lemon peel.

MAPLE LEAF

Shake together two parts bourbon, one part lemon juice and a teaspoon of maple syrup.

MERRY K

Stir two parts bourbon with one part orange curaçao and add a twist of lemon peel.

MINT JULEP

There is a delicate art to making this drink successfully: Into the glass put four or five fresh mint leaves, a tablespoon of finely ground sugar and a tablespoon of water and crush until the sugar is dissolved. Add a measure of bourbon and top up with crushed ice – which should cause the outside of the glass to frost. Decorate with a sprig of fresh mint and serve with straws.

OLD FASHIONED

Over a teaspoon of sugar in the glass shake a couple of dashes of Angostura bitters and

... that swarming million-footed, tower-masted, and sky-soaring citadel that bears the magic name of the Island of Manhattan. Thomas Wolfe

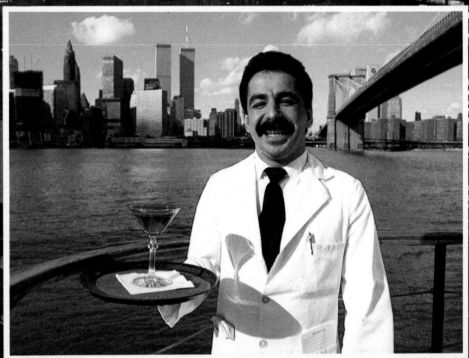

Surely the most famous of all whiskey cocktails, the stylish Manhattan is loved all over the world. A perfectly-made Manhattan should be crystal-clear and ice-cold, and is stirred, not shaken. Place five or six ice cubes in a mixing glass and add two measures of Rye whiskey, one measure of sweet red vermouth and a dash of Angostura bitters. Stir with a long-handled barspoon until the drink is well chilled – a frost will appear on the outer surface of the mixing glass – and strain into a cocktail glass. Decorate with a submerged maraschino cherry.

WHISKY BASED

Facing page: Commodore (p.68); below: Rob Roy; below left: Old Nick.

a little water. Stir to dissolve the sugar and fill the glass with ice. Top up with rye, decorate with a cherry and a twist of lemon peel or a slice of orange, and serve with a stirrer.

OLD NICK ♇

Shake together four parts rye, two parts Drambuie, one part orange juice, one part lemon juice and a couple of dashes of orange bitters. Garnish with a cherry.

OLD PAL ♇

Stir together equal parts rye, dry vermouth and Campari.

OPENING ♇

Stir two parts rye with one part sweet vermouth and one part grenadine.

ORIENTAL ♇

Shake together two parts rye, one part sweet vermouth, one part white curaçao and one part fresh lime juice.

PICCA ♇

Stir two parts Scotch with one part Galliano and one part Punt e Mes, and decorate with a cherry.

ROB ROY ♇

Stir together equal parts Scotch and sweet vermouth, and a dash of Angostura bitters. Garnish with a cherry.

ROYALIST ♇

Stir one part bourbon with two parts dry vermouth, one part Bénédictine and a dash of peach bitters.

*Right and opposite:
Shamrock; below right:
Rusty Nail; below:
Wembley; bottom:
Ward Eight.*

RUSTY NAIL

Over ice cubes pour two parts Scotch and one part Drambuie, and drop in a twist of lemon peel.

RYE LANE

Shake together equal parts rye, white curaçao and orange juice, and a couple of dashes of crème de noyau.

SHAMROCK

Stir one part Irish whiskey with one part dry vermouth, three dashes of green Chartreuse and three dashes of green crème de menthe.

SILENT THIRD

Shake together equal parts Scotch, Cointreau and lemon juice.

UP-TO-DATE

Stir two parts rye with two parts dry vermouth, one part Grand Marnier and a dash of Angostura bitters. Garnish with a twist of orange peel.

WARD EIGHT

Shake together two parts rye, one part orange juice, one part lemon juice and a teaspoon of grenadine.

WEMBLEY

Shake together equal parts Scotch, dry vermouth and pineapple juice.

WHISKY COCKTAIL

Stir four parts Scotch with one part orange curaçao and a couple of dashes of Angostura bitters. Garnish with a cherry.

WHISKY MAC

Into a glass pour three parts Scotch and two parts ginger wine.

WHISKY SOUR

Shake together three parts Scotch, two parts freshly squeezed lemon juice, one part gomme syrup and a dash of egg white. Garnish with a slice of lemon.

WHIZZ BANG

Stir two parts Scotch with one part dry vermouth, and a couple of dashes each of pastis, grenadine and orange bitters.

The cocktails illustrated here are based on various wines, including sherry, vermouth and Dubonnet. The Sherry Cobbler (far left) is made by filling a glass with crushed ice and adding sherry, orange curaçao and sugar syrup. The Americano (second from left) is a mixture of sweet vermouth and Campari topped up with soda water. Kir (third from left) is made by pouring a teaspoonful of crème de cassis into a goblet and topping up with chilled white wine. To make a Champagne Cocktail (third from right), seen here served in a sugar-frosted glass, soak a lump of sugar in Angostura bitters, add a little brandy and fill the glass with ice-cold champagne. The Spritzer (second from right) is a perfect summer drink – dry white wine and soda water; and Dubonnet, cherry brandy, orange juice, lemon juice and egg white are shaken, strained and topped up with soda water to produce a Dubonnet Fizz (far right).

WINE

'From wine what sudden friendship springs!'
John Gay.

Broadly defined as 'the fermented juice of grapes',
the term wine is used to cover sherry, port,
vermouth and other wine-based aperitifs, madeira,
champagne, sparkling wine and, of course, wine
itself. Both port and sherry are wines fortified with
brandy, port coming from the Douro valley in
Portugal, and sherry, originally, from the province
of Cadiz in Spain. Vermouth, whose name derives
from 'wermut', the German word for wormwood, is
usually based on white wine (the red being
coloured with caramel), and flavoured with
aromatic ingredients including herbs,
spices, roots and fruit peels.

WINE BASED

ADONIS ♈
Stir two parts dry sherry with one part sweet vermouth and a dash of orange bitters. Add a twist of orange peel.

ALFONSO ♈
Dissolve a lump of sugar in a couple of dashes of Angostura bitters at the bottom of the glass, add a measure of Dubonnet and top up with chilled champagne. Stir gently and add a twist of lemon peel.

AMERICANO ▭
Over ice cubes pour one part sweet

BELLINI ♈
Pour a little peach juice into the glass and top up with chilled champagne.

BLACK MAGIC ♈
Squeeze the juice of two grapes into the glass, add two dashes of Mandarine Napoléon and top with dry, sparkling wine. Drop one black grape into the drink and put another on the rim of the glass.

BLACK VELVET ▯
Into a glass pour equal parts chilled champagne and Guinness.

Below: Adonis; facing page and bottom: Black Magic; below right: Bellini; far right: Buck's Fizz.

vermouth and one part Campari. Top up with soda water and garnish with a slice of orange or a twist of lemon peel.

BAMBOO ♈
Stir one part dry sherry with one part dry vermouth and a dash of orange bitters. Add a twist of lemon peel.

BRAZIL ♈
Stir one part dry sherry with one part dry vermouth, a dash of Angostura bitters and a dash of pastis. Add a twist of lemon peel.

BUCK'S FIZZ ♈
Pour freshly squeezed orange juice into a

'The walls are hung with velvet that is black and soft as sin . . .'   G. K. Chesterton

And what could be more wicked than a tempting Black Velvet? To make the Black Velvet, sometimes called a Bismarck, half-fill a highball glass or beer tankard with chilled stout, and top up with an equal quantity of iced champagne. The proverbial pauper and aristocrat – drinks at opposite ends of a spectrum – meet and mix here very successfully.

Stout is a very dark beer which is made with a high proportion of hops and malt, roasted barley contributing added colour and flavour. The most famous stout in the world is Guinness.

Champagne is a naturally sparkling wine whose bubbles were first put there by Dom Perignon at the end of the 17th century.

Despite its cardinal sin of mixing grain and grape, Black Velvet is a deliciously smooth drink which is claimed by many to be an effective hangover remedy, if taken with breakfast.

glass and add chilled champagne in a ratio of one part orange juice to two parts champagne.

CARDINALE

Pour a little crème de cassis into a glass and top up with dry, red wine.

CHAMPAGNE COCKTAIL

Drop a lump of sugar into the glass and soak it with Angostura bitters. Add a couple of dashes of brandy and top with chilled champagne. Garnish with a slice of orange and a cherry.

CHAMPAGNE FLIP

Shake together one part fresh orange juice, three dashes of orange curaçao, a teaspoon of gomme syrup and an egg yolk. Top up with champagne.

CHAMPAGNE JULEP

Drop a lump of sugar and a couple of mint leaves into the glass and crush gently to release the mint flavour. Top up with champagne, stir and add a sprig of mint.

CHAMPAGNE NAPOLÉON

Pour a measure of Mandarine Napoléon and a dash of orange juice into the glass and top up with chilled champagne.

DUBONNET FIZZ

Shake together three parts Dubonnet, one part cherry brandy, two parts fresh orange juice, two parts fresh lemon juice and an egg white. Top up with soda water.

DUCHESS

Stir one part sweet vermouth with one part dry vermouth and one part pastis.

FINO MAC

Stir two parts dry sherry with one part ginger wine.

FRAISE ROYALE

Blend two fresh strawberries with a dash of fraise liqueur and top with chilled champagne. Stick a fresh strawberry on the rim of the glass.

GREENBRIAR

Stir two parts dry sherry with one part dry

vermouth and a dash of peach bitters. Add a sprig of mint.

HAPPY YOUTH

Drop a lump of sugar into the glass and soak it in cherry brandy. Add à measure of fresh orange juice and top with chilled champagne.

Below: Duchess; bottom: Kir; below left and facing page: Fraise Royale.

JEREZ COCKTAIL

Stir a measure of dry sherry with a dash each of orange and peach bitters, and add ice cubes.

KIR

Pour about a teaspoon of crème de cassis into the glass and fill with chilled dry white wine. Replacing the wine with champagne results in a *Kir Royale*.

WINE BASED

MERRY WIDOW FIZZ 🍷

Shake together three parts Dubonnet, one
part fresh lemon juice, one part fresh
orange juice and an egg white. Top up with
soda water.

MIMOSA 🥂

Make in the same way as Buck's Fizz, and
add a splash of orange curaçao.

PORT WINE 🍷

Stir four parts port with one part brandy
and add a twist of orange peel.

half-fill with sherry. Add a splash of orange
curaçao and a teaspoon of gomme syrup
and stir. Garnish with a sprig of mint and a
slice each of orange and lemon.

SHERRY FLIP 🍸

Shake together a measure of sherry, a
teaspoon of sugar and an egg. Grate a little
nutmeg over the top.

SHERRY TWIST 🍸

Shake together two parts dry sherry, two
parts orange juice, one part Scotch and a
couple of dashes of Cointreau.

*Above: Mimosa;
opposite: Duchess
(p.85); left and
far left: Ritz
Fizz served in The
Bar at The Ritz.*

RITZ FIZZ 🥂

Pour a dash each of amaretto, blue curaçao
and clear lemon juice into the glass, top
with chilled champagne and garnish with a
rose petal.

SHERRY COBBLER 🍷

Put plenty of crushed ice into a glass and

SPRITZER 🍷

Over two or three ice cubes pour equal
parts dry white wine and soda water. Add a
twist of lemon peel.

VERMOUTH CASSIS 🍷

Over ice cubes pour equal parts crème de
cassis and dry vermouth.

'Variety's the very spice of life' said William Cowper back in the eighteenth century, and the following mixtures undoubtedly offer variety. The Velvet Hammer (far left) is a rich, fattening concoction of Cointreau, Tia Maria and fresh double cream. The long, cooling Limbo (second from left) is a blend of peach brandy and pineapple juice served with plenty of ice. A Pimm's No. 1 (third from left) calls for, and evokes, the hot, hazy, lazy days of summer; and the aromatic, tangerine taste of Mandarine Napoléon combines deliciously with fresh orange juice in a Waterloo (third from right). An Apricot Sour (second from right) is made by shaking apricot brandy, lemon juice, Angostura bitters and sugar with a little egg white; and the Jack Rose (far right) is a mixture of lime juice, applejack brandy (or young calvados) and grenadine.

SPECIALS

The following concoctions are based on the less familiar spirits, and fruit, herb or spice-flavoured brandies and liqueurs. Fresh, minty crème de menthe, the aniseed liqueurs, Cointreau, Bénédictine and all the mystifying coloured liquids which turn up in miniature bottles at Christmastime offer the chance to experiment and create. Tequila, a relatively recent addition to the drinks cupboard, is included here, as are the virtually interchangeable calvados and applejack brandies. And coffee-flavoured Kahlua from Mexico and Tia Maria from Jamaica will happily fit each others' recipes. À votre santé!

Above: Apricot Sour; above right: Brewer Street Rascal; far right and facing page: Margarita (p.94).

AFTER DINNER ♈

Shake together equal parts of prunelle brandy, cherry brandy and lemon juice.

ANGEL'S TIP ♈

Pour three parts brown crème de cacao into the glass, and float one part cream on top.

APRICOT SOUR ♈

Shake together one part apricot brandy, two parts lemon juice, a dash of Angostura bitters, a dash of egg white and a dash of gomme syrup. Garnish with a wedge of apricot.

BANSHEE ♈

Blend together three parts white crème de cacao, three parts crème de banane, four parts cream, a dash of gomme syrup and a small scoop of crushed ice.

BENTLEY ♈

Stir one part applejack brandy with one part Dubonnet.

BLACKTHORN ♈

Stir two parts sloe gin with one part sweet vermouth and a dash of orange bitters. Add a twist of lemon peel.

BLOCK AND FALL ♈

Stir two parts Cointreau with two parts apricot brandy, one part anisette and one part applejack brandy (or calvados).

BLUE MARGARITA ♈

Shake together two parts tequila, two parts freshly squeezed lime juice and one part blue curaçao.

BRAVE BULL ♈

Over ice cubes pour equal measures of tequila and Kahlua.

BREWER STREET RASCAL ♈

Shake together one part Mandarine Napoléon, four parts grapefruit juice, a

splash of vodka and a dash of egg white. Garnish with a piece of grapefruit.

CALVADOS COCKTAIL

Shake together two parts calvados, two parts orange juice, one part Cointreau and one part orange bitters.

CLUBMAN

Shake together one part Irish Mist, four parts orange juice and a dash of egg white. Pour over ice cubes and slowly add a few drops of blue curaçao to marble the drink.

COOL BANANA

Shake together four parts crème de banane, three parts triple sec, one part grenadine, four parts double cream and a dash of egg white. Serve with fat straws.

COPPERINO

Shake together equal parts Galliano, Kahlua and cream, and dust with nutmeg.

DANISH MARY

Shake together one part akvavit, three parts tomato juice, a squeeze of fresh lemon juice, a couple of dashes of Worcestershire sauce and a pinch of celery salt. Pour over ice cubes and garnish with a slice of lemon.

DIKI DIKI

Shake together four parts calvados, one part Swedish punsch and one part grapefruit juice.

DOCTOR

Shake together two parts Swedish punsch and one part fresh lemon or lime juice.

DUKE

Shake together two parts Drambuie, one part orange juice, one part lemon juice and an egg. Pour into the glass and splash in a little champagne.

FUTURITY

Stir one part sloe gin with one part sweet vermouth and a dash of Angostura bitters.

GINGER SQUARE

Over ice cubes pour a measure of ginger brandy and stir in ginger ale to taste.

GLOOM CHASER

Shake together equal parts of Grand Marnier, white curaçao, grenadine and lemon juice.

GOLDEN CADILLAC

Shake together equal parts Galliano, white crème de cacao and fresh cream.

GOLDEN DREAM

Shake together equal parts Galliano, Cointreau, orange juice and cream.

GOLDEN SLIPPER

Shake together one part yellow Chartreuse, one part apricot brandy and an egg yolk.

GRAND SLAM

Stir two parts Swedish punsch with one part sweet vermouth and one part dry vermouth.

GRASSHOPPER

Shake together equal parts white crème de cacao, green crème de menthe and cream.

HARVARD COOLER

Shake together one part applejack brandy, the juice of a lemon (or lime), and a teaspoon of gomme syrup. Pour over ice cubes and top up with soda water.

The Grand Slam (or the winning of every trick in a hand of Bridge . . .) is pictured far left and facing page. The potent mixture, combining Swedish Punsch with sweet and dry vermouths, is served here on the rocks.

Above: the Golden Slipper is a romantic concoction – sweet and creamy.

'SPECIALS'

HARVEY COWPUNCHER

Over ice cubes pour a measure of Galliano and stir in fresh milk to taste.

HONEYMOON

Shake together one part Bénédictine, one part applejack brandy, one part lemon juice and three dashes of orange curaçao.

LONDON FOG

Shake together one part white crème de menthe, one part anisette and a dash of Angostura bitters.

MACARONI

Shake together two parts pastis and one part sweet vermouth.

Facing page and below far right: London Fog; below right: King Alfonse.

Above: a tropical Limbo – long and cool.

JACK ROSE

Shake together three parts applejack brandy, one part grenadine and the juice of half a lime.

KING ALFONSE

Pour three parts Kahlua into the glass, and float one part cream on top.

LIBERTY

Stir two parts applejack brandy with one part white rum and a dash of gomme syrup.

LIMBO

Fill the glass with ice cubes and pour in one part peach brandy and four parts pineapple juice.

MANDARINE SOUR

Shake together one part Mandarine Napoléon, one part fresh lemon juice, a dash of egg white and a dash of Angostura bitters.

MARGARITA

Shake together two parts tequila, two parts fresh lime juice and one part triple sec. Serve in a salt-frosted glass.

MISTY COOLER

Shake together one part Irish Mist, two parts lemon juice, a dash of grenadine and a dash of of egg white. Pour over ice cubes and top with soda water.

From the sparkling island of Jamaica, which sits in the azure-blue Caribbean Sea, and which Christopher Columbus considered to be 'The fairest isle that eyes have beheld,' comes a cocktail called Run Run. This concoction, as sumptuous as the surrounding landscape, was invented in the cocktail bar of the Jamaica Hilton International.

To make this cocktail, place several ice cubes in the shaker and add the following ingredients: 1¼ oz Amontillado, 1 oz crème de cacao, ½ oz overproof (extra-strong) rum, 3 oz pineapple juice and ½ oz grenadine. Shake the mixture until well chilled, strain, and serve in a large goblet.

Tropical cocktails allow plenty of scope for imaginative garnishes, such as melon, fresh pineapple, coloured cherries and pretty straws. For a truly wicked added indulgence, top the cocktail with whipped cream.

'SPECIALS'

Below: Mona Lisa; opposite: Limbo (p.94); bottom: Pimm's No. 1; below right: Moon Drops; far right: Nightcap Flip.

MOCHA MINT ♗

Shake together equal parts Kahlua, white crème de menthe and white crème de cacao. Pour over ice cubes.

MOCKINGBIRD ⊔

Over ice cubes pour one part tequila, two parts grapefruit juice and a dash of lime juice. Serve with a cherry and a stirrer.

MONA LISA ♗

Shake together one part Amer Picon, one part orange curaçao, one part Bénédictine and a teaspoon of double cream. Dust with cinnamon.

NIGHTCAP FLIP ♗

Shake together one part anisette, one part orange curaçao, one part brandy and an egg yolk.

ORANGE CADILLAC ♗

This creamy, pale orange drink is made in a blender. Blend together four parts Galliano, three parts white crème de cacao, one part fresh orange juice, four parts cream and a scoop of crushed ice.

PICON ♗

Stir one part Amer Picon with one part sweet vermouth.

MOON DROPS ♗

A speciality of the Jamaica Hilton International.
Stir 1 ounce Christian Brothers Sherry with four ounces Red Stripe Beer and strain into a cocktail glass. Garnish with a melon ball.

NAP FRAPPÉ ♗

Over plenty of crushed ice pour one part Kümmel, one part green Chartreuse and one part brandy.

PIMM'S No. 1 ⊔

A true Pimm's should not resemble an alcoholic fruit salad! Stir one part Pimm's No. 1 Cup with two or three parts lemonade, 7UP, Sprite or ginger ale. Add plenty of ice, a slice of lemon, a slice of orange, a slice of cucumber and, if available, a sprig of mint.

PINK PUSSY ⊔

Shake together two parts Campari, one part peach brandy and a dash of egg white.

Below: a striped Pousse Café; below right and opposite: Golden Dream (p.93); right: Rose.

Pour over ice cubes and top up with bitter lemon.

PISCO PUNCH

Shake together two parts pisco, one part pineapple juice, one part fresh lime juice, a couple of dashes of maraschino and a couple of dashes of gomme syrup.

POUSSE CAFÉ

A striped drink in a tall, thin glass, the Pousse Café is a true tester of the bartender's art. It consists of several coloured liqueurs, of different densities, floated one upon another, and any number between three and seven can be used. The liquids can be poured down the side of the glass or over the back of a teaspoon. There are several different combinations of which these are examples.
In the order stated pour equal quantities of the following: grenadine, crème de menthe, Galliano, Kümmel and brandy; or grenadine, Parfait Amour and maraschino. An added indulgence is a dollop of thick, sweet cream on top ...

RITZ ROYALE

Shake together equal parts peach brandy, Punt e Mes and fresh lemon juice, with a dash of gomme syrup. Strain and top up with soda water.

ROSE

Stir one part kirsch with two parts dry vermouth and a teaspoon of sirop de roses. Garnish with a cherry or a rose petal.

RUN RUN

A speciality of the Jamaica Hilton International.
Shake the following ingredients with crushed ice: 1¼ ounces Amontillado, 1 ounce crème de cacao, ½ ounce overproof rum, 3 ounces pineapple juice and ½ ounce grenadine. Do not strain, but pour into a large goblet or brandy balloon and garnish extravagantly.

SAINT GERMAIN

Shake together one part green Chartreuse, one part lemon juice, one part grapefruit juice and an egg white.

SAVOY 90

Specially concocted in 1979 to celebrate the Savoy's 90th anniversary.

Mexico 'land of great solitudes and the baroque' is the home of a species of agave plant called the agave tequilana weber, known to the locals as blue mezcal. The heart of this spiky-leaved cactus-like plant looks like a pineapple and is consequently called the pina. By distilling the juice extracted from the pina, the spirit tequila is made. This fiery spirit has only recently become popular outside its native Mexico one of the main reasons being the beautiful cocktail illustrated here: the Tequila Sunrise.

Fill a highball glass with ice-cubes and add measure of tequila and four measures of orange juice. Stir the mixture and add a little grenadine which will sink to the bottom and then gradually infuse to give the exotic sunrise effect which can be seen here. Decorate with a slice of orange and a cherry, and serve with straws and a stirrer

'SPECIALS'

Shake together 1 ounce fresh lime juice, 1 ounce amaretto and a dash of orange flower water. Strain into a sugar-frosted glass and top up with chilled champagne.

SHANNON SHANDY

Over ice cubes pour one part Irish Mist and a dash of Angostura bitters. Gently stir and top up with dry ginger ale.

SILK STOCKINGS

This drink is as smooth as it sounds, and made in a blender. Into the blender cup pour three parts tequila, two parts white crème de cacao, three parts fresh cream and a dash of grenadine. Whizz up with a scoop of crushed ice and pour the mixture into a glass. Dust with cinnamon and garnish with a cherry.

SLOE GIN COCKTAIL

Stir two parts sloe gin with one part dry vermouth and one part sweet vermouth.

SNOWBALL

Stir one part advocaat with a dash of lime juice cordial, and then gently stir in lemonade. Pour over ice cubes and garnish with a maraschino cherry.

SOURTEQ

As the name implies, a tequila sour: Shake together two parts tequila, one part fresh lemon juice, a couple of dashes of gomme syrup and a dash of egg white. Garnish with a slice of lemon and a cherry.

STARBOARD LIGHT

Shake together two parts sloe gin, one part crème de menthe and one part lemon juice.

SUISSESSE

Shake together one part pastis, one part lemon juice and an egg white. Pour into a tumbler and add a squirt of soda water.

SUNNY DREAM

Blend together two parts apricot brandy, one part Cointreau, six parts orange juice and a scoop of vanilla ice cream. Garnish with a slice of orange.

SUNRISE

Shake together two parts tequila, one part Galliano, one part crème de banane, one part cream, a dash of grenadine and a dash of lemon juice.

SUNSET

Stir two parts tequila with one part lemon juice and a teaspoon of clear honey and pour over a scoop of crushed ice.

SWISS

Shake together one part pastis, one part fresh cream and a teaspoon of grenadine.

TEMPTER

Stir one part apricot liqueur with one part port.

Opposite and above: Silk Stockings; left: Snowball.

TEQUADOR

Shake together three parts tequila, four parts pineapple juice and a dash of lime juice. Pour over crushed ice and splash with a little grenadine. Serve with straws.

TEQUILA SUNRISE

Over ice in a tall glass pour one part tequila and four parts orange juice. Stir and add two dashes of grenadine. Garnish with a slice of orange and a cherry and serve with straws.

TIDAL WAVE

Over ice cubes pour one part Mandarine Napoléon and a dash of lemon juice. Top up

'SPECIALS'

Below: Sunset (p.105); below right:
Velvet Hammer; opposite: Mona Lisa (p.98).

with bitter lemon, stir and garnish with a
slice of lemon.

TIGER'S TAIL

Over ice cubes pour one part pastis and two
parts fresh orange juice. Garnish with a
slice of orange.

VALENCIA

Shake together two parts apricot brandy,
one part orange juice and four dashes of
orange bitters. If this drink is topped up
with ice-cold champagne, it becomes a
Valencia Smile.

VELVET HAMMER

Shake together equal parts of Cointreau,
Tia Maria and fresh cream.

VIKING

Shake together three parts Swedish
punsch, one part aquavit and one part fresh
lime juice. Pour over ice cubes.

WATERLOO

Over ice in a tall glass pour one part
Mandarine Napoléon and four parts fresh
orange juice.

WINNIE-THE-POOH

Shake together four parts egg flip, one part
coffee liqueur, one part chocolate liqueur
and two parts fresh cream.

YELLOW PARROT

Stir one part pastis with one part yellow
Chartreuse and one part apricot brandy.

For anyone preferring not to drink alcohol, the following drinks succeed on three counts: they tempt the eye, they tempt the palate and they taste delicious. The Pussyfoot (far left) not only tastes good, but it is healthy too, combining orange, lemon and lime juices with egg yolk and grenadine (which adds sweetness and colour) and, here, it is made into a long drink by topping up the glass with soda water. A Jersey Lily (second from left) is basically fizzy apple juice with a dash of Angostura bitters, and the San Francisco (third from left) is another of the refreshing fruit juice and grenadine concoctions. Ice cream, fresh cream and cola add up to a Mickey Mouse (centre front), while the Capucine (third from right) is another creamy mixture, this time flavoured with peppermint and topped with grated chocolate. The Princess Margaret (second from right) is virtually a strawberry sorbet, served in a sugar-frosted glass, the rim of the glass dipped in sirop de fraise and then in granulated sugar. The marzipan-like taste of the Yellow Dwarf (far right) comes from orgeat – a non-alcoholic, almond-flavoured syrup.

MOCKTAILS

'Temperance is the noblest gift of the gods' (Euripides), and 'Temperance is the greatest of all the virtues' (Plutarch). And who are we to argue? Syrups in flavours as diverse as peach, almond, strawberry and mint, as well as a wide range of exotic fruit juices mean that mocktails can be just as exciting and delicious as their alcoholic rivals. Here is the chance to go a little bit mad with the garnishes – so let your imagination run riot!

Opposite and far right: Cinderella; below: Capucine; bottom: Acapulco Gold; right: Anita.

ACAPULCO GOLD

Shake together six parts pineapple juice, one part grapefruit juice, two parts coconut cream, two parts fresh cream and a scoop of crushed ice. Serve unstrained.

ANITA

Shake together three parts orange juice, one part lemon juice and a couple of dashes of Angostura bitters. Top with soda water, garnish with fruit and serve with straws.

APPLEADE

Chop up two large apples and pour a pint of boiling water over them. Sprinkle in about a teaspoon of sugar and leave to stand for a few minutes. Strain the liquid and leave to cool. Serve with plenty of ice and garnish with a wedge of apple and a slice of lemon.

BARLEYADE

Pour equal quantities of lemon barley and lemonade into a tumbler; add ice, a slice of lemon, and straws.

BOO BOO'S SPECIAL

Shake together equal quantities of orange juice and pineapple juice, a squeeze of lemon juice, a dash of Angostura bitters, a dash of grenadine and a scoop of crushed ice. Serve unstrained, garnish with fruit and top with a little water if desired.

CAPUCINE

Shake together one part peppermint cordial and four parts fresh cream. Strain and add crushed ice. Finely grate a little plain chocolate over the top.

CARDINAL PUNCH

Over ice cubes pour four parts cranberry juice, two parts orange juice, one part lemon juice and ginger ale to top up. Garnish with fruit and serve with straws.

CINDERELLA

Shake together equal parts pineapple juice, orange juice and lemon juice. Strain over ice cubes, top with soda water and splash in a little grenadine. Garnish with a slice of

Below: Jersey Lily (p.114) attractively garnished with a thin slice of apple.

Opposite and above far right: a Grecian – as exotic as any alcoholic concoction!

pineapple, or a pineapple chunk and a cherry on a stick, and serve with straws.

EGG NOG

Shake together a tumbler-full of milk, an egg, a teaspoon of sugar and ice. Dust with freshly-grated nutmeg, garnish with a maraschino cherry and serve with straws.

GODCHILD

Place four or five ice cubes in the glass and fill three-quarters full with lemonade. Add a squeeze of lemon juice and gently pour a measure of sirop de cassis on top. Garnish with a slice of lemon and serve with straws.

GRECIAN

Blend together four parts peach juice, two parts orange juice, one part lemon juice and a scoop of crushed ice. Pour unstrained into the glass, add a squirt of soda water and garnish with fresh fruit.

HIMBEERSAFT

Fill the glass with crushed ice, pour in a measure of sirop de framboise and dilute with soda water. The quantities of each will depend upon individual taste. Stir well, garnish with a sprig of mint and serve with straws.

MOCKTAILS

Below: Lemonade (Golden); facing page: Jersey Lily; bottom: Mock Daisy Crusta; far right: a summery Surfer's Paradise (p.118).

HORSEFEATHERS

Over ice cubes pour consommé and flavour with Tabasco and Worcestershire sauce to taste, a good squeeze of lemon juice and a pinch of salt. Stir thoroughly and garnish with a stick of celery which will also serve as a stirrer.

JERSEY LILY

Stir a glass of fizzy apple juice with a little sugar, a dash of Angostura bitters and ice cubes. Strain and garnish with a maraschino cherry.

KEELPLATE

Shake together two parts tomato juice, one part clam juice, a couple of dashes of Worcestershire sauce and a good pinch of celery salt.

LEMONADE (FIZZY)

Pour the juice of a lemon into the glass and add two teaspoons of sugar. Stir until the sugar is dissolved, add four or five ice cubes and top up with soda water. Garnish with a slice of lemon.

LEMONADE (GOLDEN)

Shake together the juice of a lemon, a wine-glass of water, an egg yolk and two teaspoons of sugar. Strain into the glass, add ice cubes and garnish with fruit.

LEMONADE (PINK)

Make in the same way as still lemonade (below) and stir in a tablespoon of sirop de framboise.

LEMONADE (STILL)

Shake together two scoops of crushed ice, the juice of a lemon and two teaspoons of sugar. Pour, unstrained, into the glass and top up with water. Garnish with a slice of lemon and serve with straws.

LEMON ICE CREAM SODA

Put two tablespoons of fresh lemon juice in a glass with two teaspoons of sugar and stir until the sugar is dissolved. Fill the glass two-thirds full with soda water and top with a large scoop of soft vanilla ice cream. Serve with straws and a spoon. Similarly, orange or grapefruit versions can be made.

LIMEADE

Shake together the juice of three limes and sugar to taste. Strain over ice cubes and add water or soda water. Garnish with fruit.

LIMEY

Shake together two parts lime juice, one part lemon juice and half an egg white. Garnish with a cherry.

MICKEY MOUSE

Over ice cubes pour cola, then add a scoop of soft vanilla ice cream, top with whipped cream and two cherries, and serve with straws and a spoon.

MOCK DAISY CRUSTA

Put two scoops of crushed ice into the glass and add the juice of two limes and a tablespoon of sirop de framboise. Top up with soda water and float a little grenadine on top. Garnish with a sprig of mint and raspberries on a stick.

NURSERY FIZZ

Over ice cubes pour equal parts orange juice and ginger ale. Garnish with a slice of orange and a cherry and serve with straws.

114

MOCKTAILS

Below: Redcurrant and Lemon; facing page: Acapulco Gold (p.110); far right: Parson's Particular; below right: a frothy, appetising Pom Pom.

PARSON'S PARTICULAR

Shake together two parts fresh orange juice, one part fresh lemon juice, an egg yolk and four dashes of grenadine. Strain and garnish with a cherry.

PARSON'S SPECIAL

Shake together a large measure of orange juice, an egg yolk and four dashes of grenadine. Strain and top up with soda water.

POM POM

Shake together the juice of half a lemon, an egg white and a dash of grenadine. Strain over crushed ice, top up with lemonade and garnish with a slice of lemon.

PONCE

Over two scoops of crushed ice pour four parts pineapple juice, one part grenadine, one part orgeat syrup and one part passion fruit juice. Stir in soda to top up.

PRINCESS MARGARET

Blend together five or six strawberries, a slice of pineapple, the juice of half a lemon, juice of half an orange, a couple of dashes of sirop de fraise and a scoop of crushed ice. Pour into a sugar-frosted glass (stick the sugar with sirop de fraise rather than egg white or gomme), and garnish with a strawberry on the rim.

PUSSYFOOT

Shake together equal parts orange juice, lemon juice and lime juice, along with a dash of grenadine and an egg yolk. Add soda water if desired, garnish with a cherry and serve with straws.

QUEEN CHARLIE

Over ice cubes pour a measure of grenadine and top up with soda water. Garnish with a slice of lemon and a cherry on a stick, and serve with straws.

REDCURRANT AND LEMON

Heat one tablespoon of redcurrant jelly with two tablespoons of water to dissolve. Add the juice of a lemon and stir. Pour over ice cubes and top up with either soda water or water. Garnish with a slice of lemon.

ROSY PIPPIN

Stir a wine glass of apple juice with a dash of grenadine and a squeeze of lemon juice. Top up with ginger ale and garnish with a wedge of apple.

Top: Shirley Temple; above: San Francisco; above right: Southern Belle; facing page: Temperance.

SAINT CLEMENTS

The name derives from the children's nursery rhyme "Oranges and lemons say the bells of Saint Clements…" and the drink is made by stirring equal parts of orange juice and bitter lemon with plenty of ice. Serve garnished with slices of orange and lemon.

SAN FRANCISCO

Shake together equal parts orange juice, lemon juice, grapefruit juice and pineapple juice, along with an egg white and a dash of

grenadine. Top up with soda water and garnish extravagantly!

SHIRLEY TEMPLE

Over ice cubes pour ginger ale and add a little grenadine. Stir and garnish with a cherry.

SOUTHERN BELLE

A non-alcoholic Mint Julep…Crush a sprig of mint with a teaspoon of sugar at the bottom of a glass, to extract the mint flavour. Add a squeeze of lemon juice and lots of ice. Top up with ginger ale, garnish with a sprig of mint and serve with straws.

SUMMERTIME SODA

Stir the juice of an orange with the juice of a lemon and the juice of a grapefruit. Pour over ice cubes and add soda water and a scoop of soft vanilla ice cream. Serve with straws and a spoon.

SURFER'S PARADISE

Over ice cubes pour the juice of half a lime and three dashes of Angostura bitters. Stir in lemonade to top up and garnish with a slice of orange.

TEMPERANCE

Shake together the juice of a lemon, a couple of dashes of grenadine and an egg yolk. Garnish with a cherry.

TOMATO JUICE COCKTAIL

Shake together tomato juice, a good squeeze of lemon juice, a couple of dashes of Worcestershire sauce, a couple of drops of Tabasco, a pinch of celery salt and a shake of pepper. Strain and serve straight up or on the rocks. Garnish with a slice of lemon and a stick of celery.

UGLY

The ugli fruit resembles a cross between a grapefruit and an orange, and this drink is made up of equal quantities of grapefruit and orange juices poured over plenty of ice and served with straws.

YELLOW DWARF

Shake together one part orgeat syrup, one part cream and an egg yolk. Strain and add soda water to taste. Garnish with a maraschino cherry.

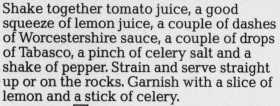

Having decided to throw a cocktail party, where do you begin? Firstly decide on a date which allows you to issue invitations about a month in advance. Then you can be fairly sure that the guests you invite will be able to come. Aim for a guest list of between ten and twenty people. This will enable you to talk to everyone and to serve drinks without panicking. The room will also feel pleasantly populated but not overcrowded.

A cocktail party traditionally takes place in the early part of the evening and invitations might suggest 'Cocktails 6.30 to 8.30 pm.' If you indicate time limits, people will not arrive expecting a full meal, and can, if they wish, make plans for the remainder of the evening.

One of the main ingredients of a successful party is a relaxed host and/or hostess, which simply involves a little careful planning. Avoid spending the party stuck behind the bar mixing drinks by limiting the number of cocktails on offer and preparing a couple of ready-mixed jugs just before the party begins. You will need plenty of ice, and at least two glasses per person. Medium-sized wine goblets and heavy-bottomed tumblers will cover almost everything, and the goblets can be hired from most wine merchants. Provide at least one appetising non-alcoholic concoction – you will be surprised at the number of people who ask for a soft drink.

A well-organised bar is essential for the smooth-flowing production of drinks. A table covered with a clean, pressed white sheet serves very well, and the space underneath is useful for bottles and boxes for the empties. Don't clutter the bar with dishes of food but do provide an ashtray for people waiting for drinks as well as plenty of other ashtrays strategically placed around the room. Protect surfaces with table cloths or drinks coasters and remove serving dishes as they are emptied.

FOOD

Cocktail snacks should ideally be bite-sized and easy to pick up. Olives (stuffed and plain), peanuts and salted cashews, gherkins, savory biscuits and crisps involve no preparation and are very popular.

Presentation of food is almost as important as taste. Serve nuts and olives in pretty bowls, and lay out canapés on smallish plates – nothing looks worse than a large platter with one or two remaining snacks. Ham and asparagus rolls are perfect on a bed of lettuce leaves, and hot foods should be served on warm plates which help retain the heat and minimise the likelihood of any surplus fat solidifying.

The following foods are attractive to the eye, simply prepared, and easy and delicious to eat. I have avoided foods made with pastry as they are relatively complicated to prepare and have a tendency to crumble.

Dips can be served with small savory biscuits and crudités. By far the most popular crudité vegetable is carrot, peeled and sliced lengthways. Add colour and variety with cauliflower florets, celery sticks, green pepper, cucumber, radishes and spring onions.

CHEESE DIP

½ lb (225g) Edam, grated
One cup top of the milk
One small onion, grated
Three teaspoons tomato purée
Two tbsps. finely chopped walnuts (optional)
Salt and pepper

Thoroughly mix cheese and milk, adding milk a little at a time. Add remaining ingredients to the creamy cheese mixture and stir until well mingled. Do not chill or the mixture will be too stiff for a dip.

CHIVE DIP

¼ lb (125g) cream cheese or curd cheese
Two tablespoons fresh chopped chives
Milk

Mix cheese and chives thoroughly and add a little milk, stirring well to achieve dipping consistency.

CURRY DIP

Two teaspoons curry powder
Two teaspoons olive oil
Two teaspoons lemon or lime juice
¼ pint sour cream,
¼ pint whipping cream
Salt

Sauté curry powder in olive oil for about five minutes on a low heat. Allow to cool and stir in sour cream, lemon/lime juice and a couple of pinches of salt. Beat up the whipping cream until it forms peaks and fold it into the mixture. This dip is especially good served with prawns or shrimps and fresh grapefruit and orange segments on sticks.

PINEAPPLE BACON

One can pineapple chunks
Thinly sliced streaky bacon, rind removed

Wrap a thin strip of bacon around each piece of pineapple and secure with wooden (not plastic) cocktail sticks. Bake in the oven until the bacon is crisp and serve hot.
A delicious variation on this theme is made in the same way, replacing the pineapple with canned, smoked oysters.

COCKTAIL PARTIES

SMOKY BACON DIP

Four rashers smoked bacon, rind removed
One 7 oz (200g) can pineapple, drained
½ lb (225g) cream cheese or curd cheese
Milk,
Paprika to garnish

Grill the bacon until really crisp and leave to cool. Mash pineapple finely and crumble the bacon between your fingers. Thoroughly mix cream cheese, bacon crumbs and pineapple, and add a little milk, if necessary, to achieve dipping consistency. Transfer to serving dish and dust with paprika.

CANAPÉS

Canapés on biscuit or toast bases tend to go soggy if left for long, so make as near the time of serving as possible. One longer-lasting base is thinly-sliced white bread fried until crisp in a little butter. Top bases decoratively with cream cheese and stuffed olives, paté and tiny wedges of tomato, slivers of smoked fish sprinkled with paprika – in fact anything appetising and attractive to the eye.

HAM AND ASPARAGUS ROLLS

½ lb (225g) sliced ham (square slices)
One can asparagus spears

Cut slices of ham in half diagonally to make triangles and roll around asparagus. Secure with cocktail sticks.

SHRIMP DIP

One 5 oz (150g) can shrimps, drained
One teaspoon ground ginger
½ teaspoon chilli powder
One onion, roughly chopped
Two tablespoons lemon juice
Four tablespoons milk
One egg
½ lb (225g) Edam or Cheddar,
grated or roughly chopped
One teaspoon dry mustard
One teaspoon sugar
½ teaspoon salt,
Pinch of black pepper
Sunflower or vegetable oil

Into the blender cup break the egg and add sugar, mustard, lemon juice, salt and pepper. Blend for about ten seconds. Then, through the hole in the lid, pour a steady trickle of oil until the mixture thickens (about ¼ pint). Then add the onion, shrimps, cheese, ginger, chilli and milk. Blend again until well mixed. This dip is best served well chilled and can be prepared a day or two in advance.

TUNA FISH DIP
and
CRABMEAT DIP

are made in exactly the same way replacing the shrimps with either a can of tuna fish or a can of crabmeat. Omit the ginger and the chilli, and add plenty of fresh-ground black pepper and a little grated lemon zest.

COCKTAIL MUSHROOMS

Sauté canned button mushrooms in butter and serve hot on cocktail sticks.

QUICK ONION DIP

One packet of onion soup mix
½ lb (225g) cream cheese
Fresh ground black pepper
Two tablespoons milk

Tip contents of soup packet into a mixing bowl and add milk. Stir to a paste and, with a fork, thoroughly mix in the cream cheese. Add pepper to taste and refrigerate until an hour before required. Prepare this dip at least two or three hours before you intend to serve it. If, before serving, the dip seems a little stiff, thin to dipping consistency by beating in a little cream.

AVOCADO DIP

Two ripe (soft) avocados
One small onion, grated
Two tablespoons sour cream or mayonnaise
One teaspoon horseradish relish
Lemon juice
Salt

Make this dip at the last minute as avocado turns dark on exposure to the air – a few drops of lemon juice helps prevent this. Peel, stone and mash the avocados. Mix all the ingredients into a smooth paste and add salt to taste.

These pages: Hangover cures are, generally speaking, somewhat unappetising – to the unfortunate victim in particular!

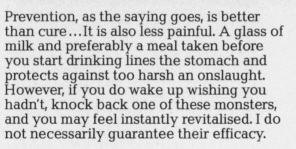

Facing page and far right: Pick-Me-Up; above: the Savoy Corpse Reviver; above right: Corpse Reviver Cocktail.

Prevention, as the saying goes, is better than cure…It is also less painful. A glass of milk and preferably a meal taken before you start drinking lines the stomach and protects against too harsh an onslaught. However, if you do wake up wishing you hadn't, knock back one of these monsters, and you may feel instantly revitalised. I do not necessarily guarantee their efficacy.

BULLSHOT

Shake together one part vodka, four parts condensed consommé or beef bouillon, a couple of dashes of Worcestershire sauce, a dash of lemon juice and a pinch of celery salt. Add Tabasco and pepper to taste.

CORPSE REVIVER COCKTAIL

Shake together one part brandy, four parts milk, a teaspoon of sugar or gomme syrup and a dash of Angostura bitters. Top up with soda water.

PICK-ME-UP

Stir one part cognac with one part pastis and one part dry vermouth.

PRAIRIE HEN

Into a small goblet pour a couple of dashes of vinegar and two teaspoons of Worcestershire sauce. Carefully break a whole egg into the glass without breaking the yolk, sprinkle with pepper and salt, and splash with a little Tabasco. Drink in one gulp.

PRAIRIE OYSTER

Into a small tumbler pour a teaspoon of Worcestershire sauce and a teaspoon of tomato sauce. Stir, and then gently add a whole, unbroken egg yolk. Splash with a little vinegar and dust with pepper. Drink in one gulp.

SAVOY CORPSE REVIVER

Shake together equal parts Fernet Branca, brandy and white crème de menthe.

Absinthe Very strong, dry, bitter liqueur with a predominantly aniseed flavour.

Advocaat Thick, sweet, yellow egg yolk and grape brandy liqueur from Holland.

Almond see *Amandes (crème de), Amaretto, Falernum, Noyau (crème de), Orgeat.*

Amandes (crème de) Sweet almond liqueur.

Amaretto Sweet almond-flavoured liqueur made with apricot kernels.

Amer Picon French branded aperitif with a hint of orange and gentian.

Amontillado Medium sherry with a dark gold colour.

Angostura Rum based bitters used sparingly to flavour many mixed drinks.

Anis Aniseed-flavoured liqueur.

Anisette Sweetened aniseed liqueur.

Aperitif Pre-meal drink, taken with a view to whetting the appetite (Latin *aperire:* to open).

Applejack Apple brandy, similar to *Calvados.*

Apricot brandy Apricot-flavoured liqueur.

Aquavit (or akvavit) Strong, colourless spirit flavoured with caraway and other ingredients.

Armagnac French grape brandy.

Aurum Italian orange-flavoured liqueur.

Bacardi Brand of white rum.

Banane (crème de) Banana liqueur.

Bénédictine Liqueur formulated in 1510 by Bénédictine monks, containing 27 flavourings extracted from fruit peels, herbs and roots.

Bitters General term for bitter essences used in many mixed drinks.

Bourbon Distinctive American whiskey made with grain – over half of which must be corn – and aged in charred oak barrels.

Brandy Spirit distilled from fruit – generally applies to grape distillates.

Brut Dry champagne.

Byrrh French branded aperitif, dry with a hint of orange and quinine.

Cacao (crème de) Very sweet chocolate and vanilla flavoured liqueur, either colourless or dark brown.

Calvados Apple brandy from Normandy, France which is known locally as *le trou Normand* because, taken between courses, the drink burns a 'hole' in the stomach, making room for the next course!

Campari Branded Italian aperitif, brilliant pink-red in colour, with a bittersweet flavour.

Cassis (crème de) Blackcurrant liqueur from the Burgundy region of France.

Cassis (sirop de) Non-alcoholic blackcurrant syrup.

Champagne A sparkling wine produced in the Champagne region of France. The sparkle is achieved by a procedure called the *méthode champenoise,* a time-consuming and expensive business which influences the price of champagne.

Champagne Cognac French grape brandy from the Cognac region of France.

Chartreuse Aromatic liqueur available in yellow or green. Green Chartreuse is said to contain 130 herbs and spices and the formula is a closely-guarded secret. The drink was invented by the Carthusian brotherhood of monks in the 16th century, and production is still presided over by monks.

Cheri Suisse Swiss chocolate-and-cherry liqueur.

Cherry brandy Cherry-flavoured liqueur.

Cinzano Brand of Italian vermouth.

Coconut liqueur White rum flavoured with coconut essences eg. Cocoribe and Malibu.

Cognac French grape brandy from the Cognac region. To qualify as a Cognac, the liquor must be distilled twice and then aged in oak for a minimum of two years.

Cointreau Brand of triple-sec curaçao. A colourless orange-flavoured liqueur which comes in a distinctive dark brown, square-shaped bottle.

Curaçao General term covering all orange-flavoured liqueurs. Triple-sec curaçao is a colourless liquor flavoured with the peel of green oranges which grow on the West Indies island of Curaçao. The liquor is sweetened and can be coloured orange, green and blue. The colour does not affect the flavour.

Digestif An after-dinner drink taken with a view to aiding the digestion.

Drambuie A distinguished whisky liqueur made from Highland malt whisky and heather honey.

Dubonnet French branded aperitif of the vermouth-type available in red or white varieties.

Falernum Almond-flavoured liqueur from Barbados.

Falernum syrup An almond, ginger and lime flavoured syrup, milky in colour.

Fernet-Branca Bitter Italian digestif, popularly thought to be an efficacious hangover cure.

Fino A pale, dry sherry.

Forbidden Fruit Strong, sweet liqueur made with grapefruit, orange and honey.

Fraises (crème de) Strawberry-coloured and flavoured liqueur.

Fraises (sirop de) Non-alcoholic strawberry syrup.

Framboises (crème de) Raspberry liqueur.

Framboises (sirop de) Raspberry syrup.

Galliano An Italian liqueur with a golden colour, flavoured with herbs and a hint of vanilla.

Genever (or Jenever) Dutch gin.

Glen Mist A whisky-based Scottish liqueur flavoured with herbs, spices and honey.

Gin Juniper-flavoured spirit. See *London Dry gin.*

Golden rum Spirit distilled from sugar cane and matured for three years in charred oak casks, with additional caramel. The liquor is a warm golden colour and it has a fuller flavour than white rum.

Gomme A sugar syrup used to sweeten many mixed drinks. (See page 9 to make your own sugar syrup.)

Grand Marnier A French orange curaçao available in two strengths, the yellow ribbon being less alcoholic than the red.

Grappa A fiery spirit distilled from the pips, stalks and skins of grapes.

Grenadine Pomegranate syrup with a distinctive orange-red colour.

Irish Mist Irish whiskey-based liqueur flavoured with Irish heather honey and herbs.

Irish whiskey A distinctive spirit whose flavour is achieved by using subtle combinations of grain, and a triple distillation process.

Jamaican rum A dark, full-bodied spirit distilled from sugar, aged in oak casks for five or more years and darkened with added caramel.

Kahlua A sweet coffee liqueur which originated in Mexico. Similar to the Jamaican *Tia Maria*.

Kirsch A French brandy distilled from cherries with a strong, dry flavour. German and Swiss versions are called *Kirschwasser.*

Kümmel A colourless distillate of grain or potato, sweetened and flavoured with caraway seeds.

Light rum A light-bodied white or golden rum.

Lillet French branded aperitif of the vermouth type, with a dry, delicate taste.

London Dry gin A neutral spirit which has been redistilled with juniper berries, coriander and a combination of ingredients collectively known as 'botanicals'.

Madeira Fortified wine with a caramel flavour.

Malt whisky Scottish distillate of malted barley.

Mandarine Napoléon Tangerine-flavoured liqueur.

Manzanilla Very dry, almost salty, sherry.

Maraschino A colourless liqueur made with Marasca cherries and their stones. The flavour is reminiscent of marzipan.

Menthe (crème de) Sweet mint liqueur available in green or white varieties. The colour makes no difference to the flavour.

Metaxa Greek brandy.

Noisettes (crème de) Hazelnut liqueur.

Noyau (crème de) Almond-flavoured pink or colourless liqueur made, not with almonds, but with peach and apricot kernels. (*Noyau* means fruit stone.)

Oloroso Sweet, dark sherry, the colour of caramel.

Orange bitters A sharp, bitter, tangy essence used in minute quantities to give a hint of orange to several mixed drinks.

Orange liqueurs See *Aurum, Cointreau, Curaçao, Grand Marnier, Triple Sec.*

Orgeat Non-alcoholic, almond-flavoured syrup.

Ouzo Colourless, aniseed-flavoured liquor from Greece. Usually served with water and/or ice, which turn the liquid a cloudy white.

Parfait Amour Literally 'perfect love', this liqueur is either violet or pink, flavoured with flower petals, citrus oils and spices.

Pastis French liquorice-flavoured liqueur, caramel brown in colour. When water is added the liquid turns a pale, cloudy yellow.

Peach bitters Peach-flavoured bitter essence.

Pernod Famous French brand of *Pastis*.

Perrier Sparkling spring water.

Pimm's No. 1 Cup Gin, flavoured with a unique combination of herbs and liqueurs used as the base

for a long, summery drink.

Pisco South American muscat grape brandy.

Port Portuguese fortified wine of which ruby is a rich, crimson colour and tawny is tinged with brown. White port, made with white grapes, is also available and drunk as an aperitif.

Prunelle Brandy distilled from sloe berries.

Punt e Mes Brand of Italian vermouth, brownish-red in colour, with a bittersweet flavour.

Roses (crème de) Delicate, flowery liqueur flavoured with rose petals, citrus oils and vanilla.

Roses (sirop de) Non-alcoholic, rose-flavoured syrup.

Royal Mint Chocolate liqueur Sweet English liqueur flavoured with peppermint and chocolate.

Rum A spirit which is distilled either from fermented sugar-cane juice or from molasses. There are several varieties of rum which differ in colour and flavour.

Rye Distinctive whiskey from the United States made from grain, over half of which must be rye. The distillate is aged in charred oak barrels for at least a year.

Saké Japanese rice liquor which is traditionally served hot.

Sambuca Strong, sweet, liquorice-flavoured liqueur from Italy traditionally served flaming with two or three coffee beans floating on top. (*Sambuca Negra* is dark brown and flavoured with coffee.)

Scotch Generalised term for blended Scottish whisky.

Sekt German sparkling white wine.

Sherry Wine, fortified with brandy, produced by a complicated method originally in Spain. The name 'sherry' applies to a similar drink now produced in many wine-growing countries. See *Amontillado, Fino, Manzanilla, Oloroso.*

Sloe gin Liqueur made by steeping sloe berries in gin.

Southern Comfort American whiskey-based liqueur flavoured with peaches.

Spumante Italian sparkling wine.

Strega Sweet, golden, Italian liqueur flavoured with more than 70 herbs, fruits and spices.

Swedish Punsch A potent blend of rum, aquavit, wine and syrup.

Tequila Spirit distilled from a cactus-like plant with spiky leaves, indigenous to Mexico.

Tia Maria A Jamaican rum-based coffee liqueur similar in taste to *Kahlua.*

Triple Sec White curaçao.

Van der Hum South African tangerine-flavoured liqueur.

Vanille (crème de) Vanilla-flavoured liqueur.

Vermouth Wine-based aperitif of which there are many patented varieties, especially from Italy and France. Available in dry or sweet versions, and in red, white and, more recently, rosé.

Violette (crème de) Scented liqueur made with violet petals.

Vodka Colourless grain distillate to which *no* flavourings are added.

Whisk(e)y Spirit distilled from grain. See *Bourbon, Irish whiskey, Malt whisky, Rye, Scotch.*

White rum Colourless, light-bodied rum of which *Bacardi* is a well-known brand.

INDEX

INDEX

ACKNOWLEDGEMENTS

The publishers wish to thank the following people and organisations for their help in the production of this book:

Benson's, Golders Green; The Black Horse, Marylebone High Street; Dino Carnota, The R.A.C. Club, Pall Mall, London (for mixing cocktails); Coconut Grove, London W.1.; Cutty Sark (U.K. Scotch Whisky) Ltd.; Fourcroy (U.K.) Ltd.; The Hammersmith Palais; International Distillers & Vintners Ltd.; The Jamaica Hilton International, Jamaica, W.I.; Jacky Laugenie, General Manager, Trader Vic's, London; Malden Golf Club, New Malden, Surrey; Martini & Rossi Ltd.; Moët & Chandon (London) Ltd.; Mike Pearson; Pimm's Ltd.; Nick Ramundi (for mixing cocktails); J.B. Reynier Ltd.; The Ritz Hotel, London; The Royal Oak, New Malden, Surrey; Saccone & Speed Ltd., Aylesbury, Bucks.; The Sand Bar, Bandos Island, Republic of the Maldives; The Savoy Hotel, London; The Scotch Whisky Association; and special thanks to the United Kingdom Bartenders' Guild.

Casablanca (page 47) served in the River Room by kind permission of the Savoy Hotel, London.
Dry Martini (page 30) served in the classic setting of The Bar at The Ritz.
Ritz Fizz (page 87) served by kind permission of the U.K. Bartenders' Guild, The Bar at The Ritz.
Ritz Royale (page 100) created by Geoffrey Glockler, Head Bartender, Ritz Casino, London.
Jewellery (pages 30 and 87) by Carrington, Old Bond Street, London.

Picture credits:

All photographs by Peter Barry, with the exception of the following:-
Clive Friend F.I.I.P. pages 4-5, 8, 10-11, 22-23, 44-45, 56-57, 66-67, 78-79, 88-89, 108-109.
Paul Kenward: pages 72-73
Neil Sutherland: pages 9, 26, 30, 37, 47, 58, 76 below right, 87 left, 92, 105 left, 116 top, 122 top left.
Chris Thomson: pages 1, 48, 51, 102-103, 114 right.

First published in Great Britain 1982 by Colour Library International Ltd.

© 1982 Illustrations and text: Colour Library International Ltd., New Malden, Surrey, England.

Colour separations by FER-CROM, Barcelona, Spain.
Display and text filmsetting by ACESETTERS LTD., Richmond, Surrey, England.
Printed and bound in Barcelona, Spain by JISA–RIEUSSET and EUROBINDER.

ISBN 0 86283 013 3

COLOUR LIBRARY INTERNATIONAL